WHEN TRUTH IS PROCLAIMED, ACTION IS REQUIRED

Therefore

— there ⟶ fore —

*Therefore ... let us throw off everything that
hinders ... let us run with perseverance....
Let us fix our eyes on Jesus.... Heb. 12:1-2*

Kay Bascom

OlivePress
צהר זית

Printed in the USA
ISBN 978-1-941173-21-3

Published by
Olive Press Messianic and Christian Publisher
www.olivepresspublisher.org
olivepressbooks@gmail.com

The author's website: www.messiahmysteryresources.org

Our prayer at Olive Press is that we may help make the Word of Adonai fully known, that it spread rapidly and be glorified everywhere. We hope our books help open people's eyes so they will turn from darkness to Light and from the power of the adversary to God and to trust in ישוע Yeshua (Jesus). (From II Thess. 3:1; Col. 1:25; Acts 26:18,15 NRSV *New Revised Standard Version* and CJB, the Complete Jewish Bible.)

Cover background images from Bing.com/images

All Scriptures, unless otherwise indicated, are taken from the *New International Version* (NIV). Copyright © 1973, 1978, 1984 by International Bible Society. Used by permission of Zondervan Publishing House. All rights reserved.
(Note that the later 2011 revision is what most online and app versions are, but the author used her own 1984 copy for this book.)

Scriptures marked NIV 2011 are taken from THE HOLY BIBLE, NEW INTERNATIONAL VERSION®, NIV®. Copyright © 1973, 1978, 1984, 2011 by Biblica, Inc.® Used by permission. All rights reserved worldwide.

Scriptures marked RSV are taken from the *Revised Standard Version* of the Bible, copyright © 1946, 1952, and 1971 the Division of Christian Education of the National Council of the Churches of Christ in the United States of America.

Scriptures marked CJB are Taken from the *Complete Jewish Bible* by David H. Stern. Copyright © 1998. All rights reserved. Used by permission of Messianic Jewish Publishers, 6120 Day Long Lane, Clarksville, Maryland 21029.

For Charles

FOREWORD

Realistic assessment. We could well be living at the conclusion of our world's history. Suspecting today to be such a pivotal time is not wide-eyed speculation. It is wide-eyed realism. The Word of God has warned us from Genesis to Revelation that history as we know it will come to an end. The world's civilization and the world's inhabitants will reach the Day of God's judgment. Multiple harbingers are pointing to a time of reckoning, signs which the prophets and the Lord Jesus predicted. The Day is guaranteed, and will bring judgment for some, and blessed fulfillment for others.

God's final goal. The *Therefore* studies are designed to help us look at salvation history as a unified story. "Salvation history" refers to God's intervention to save all who will accept His deliverance from disaster. The Old and New Testaments are an indivisible disclosure of God's dealings with humanity as He progresses toward His goal. In His Book of Revelation, Jesus tells us that justice will finally be done. Furthermore, there is to be a glorious new Heaven and new earth, replacing strife, evil, and hate with peace, righteousness, and love. Who wouldn't welcome such a Day?

"Watch!" *Therefore* is meant to alert us to our own chapter in the world's redemptive history, which is in the process of being completed, and perhaps quite soon. God's Word repeatedly throughout the ages has warned, predicted outcomes, fulfilled predictions, and offered continual mercy and grace. Yet "the Day" is perpetually held before us, a Day that will finally, and must, come. Our Lord Jesus repeatedly told us to watch, pray, be on guard, and look with eagerness for His return and all that His Second Coming would mean. We are advised to be aware, engaged, watchful, prepared, and expectant. *Therefore* is meant to awaken, inform, assure, and encourage, while there is yet time in history, or time in any individual's life. Today when wrongheadedness is rampant, confusion is epidemic, and the world's stability is teetering, it would be foolish to ignore or deny the precariousness of the hour. The whole world and each of us may soon have to give our personal account to our Maker.

21st Century precariousness. Our generation is in a particularly dangerous position. We have the benefit of having the whole Word of God available to us, and in thousands of languages. If we have not researched what God has told us, if we've ignored or summarily rejected it, we are without excuse. If we have at least given lip service to God, we need to be in a "therefore" mode. That is, what is it that we do *know* from God, so that we can *believe* it, and if we believe Him, what therefore follows, to *act* upon? Now is a time to persevere in the "therefores" which the Spirit of God has put in writing for us. God's message to us in writing is an amazing gift. It preserves the facts of life in one volume for every generation. We have been given God's pattern: there (what truth proceeded?) fore (what action or obedience, then follows?). Put symbolically: ←there + fore → That is, based on what I know and then believe, how therefore do I live it out, to God's glory?

The Bible's progression. What has God revealed about the beginning, the middle, and the end of the story of God's love affair with His creation? Although the Bible is a big body of work, it is only one volume, containing many chapters of one story that God has revealed to us in the Old and New Testaments' inseparable disclosure. This interwoven story starts at the creation of the world and progresses to God's redemptive goal, when the world will be renewed. We need to see the Scriptures as a whole, united by the Spirit of God who inspired its writers to reveal what God wanted to say to the sons and daughters of Adam. We need a panoramic mindset to explore its riches historically, redemptively, theologically, and experientially.

History's progression. Since the Fall with its entrance of sin and death, man has been engaged in a spiritual battle between Light and Darkness throughout history. The Old Testament records God's love for Israel, and her failure to repent, in microcosm. The New Testament reveals His love for His whole world—a world that has largely failed to repent, in macrocosm. Spiritual battles have raged over the world's nations and tribes throughout the ages. Within those larger battles, all human beings have lived out their own spiritual losses or victories—whether they knew they were in a cosmic battle, or not.

Our personal progression. We are deeply blessed with the presence of both the written and the living Word of God. The age of God's grace has extended for two millennia after our Lord's Incarnation. While many have come to faith, Christendom's history is checkered with apostasy and unfaithfulness over the ages. Our own generation is called to live out our Lord's life in today's world, a world oppressed by the Great Deceiver on one battlefield after another, including our own hearts. God's Word assures us of His ultimate victory in the end, which will be a new beginning. That being so, therefore, "what sort of men and women ought we to be?"

Ω

Table of Contents

STUDY SUGGESTIONS

DEAR READERS, LEADERS, AND GROUPS WHO STUDY TOGETHER, May this study bless you! Just as I've worked on it leaning on the Holy Spirit's guidance, may you interact with it by His Spirit's guidance, as well. Words on paper are dead, unless He enlivens. May your understanding be deepened, your joy increased, and your endurance strengthened as you depend upon the Spirit of God to take you on this adventure!

<u>Suggestions as you look to our Lord for these studies' usefulness:</u>

1. Bathe your study of His Word in "listening" prayer. Heart and mind connections to God's purposes and Godly responses are the goal, not information.
2. Glean what the Spirit reveals and enlivens to you, and let the rest go. He is the study's real teacher.
3. Value the fellowship of those who commit to studying together. Pray for each other.
4. Resist the enemy's discouragement and keep your eye on God's marvelous goal.
5. Focus on the Person of Jesus, *Yeshua,* the Messiah. (His Hebrew name is sometimes used in these studies, to help us visualize His Jewish context while on earth.) Be present to our Lord when He appears in Scripture, feeling the scene with your five senses and your heart.
6. Use the ♥ - marked entries to engage your will with your mind and heart.
7. Consider committing to memory the key Scriptures at the close of each study. The collection is supplied in Appendix E.

EXPLANATIONS RELATED TO THE TEXT

<u>Viewpoint:</u> Like various vitamins that our bodies need, believers' minds and spirits need all kinds of studies—book studies, subject studies, word studies, theological grounding, devotional inspiration, application-based encouragements, etc. *Therefore's* panoramic orientation is meant to help us grasp the big picture of God's purposes, how He has interacted with humanity, how He has provided for our redemption, how He indwells His people, and to what goal He is bringing us.

Progression: *Therefore* roughly moves from Genesis to Revelation, adding observations from the sweep of AD history to today. The studies begin with the basic truths of the Old Testament, move to the Incarnation, the giving of the Holy Spirit to believers, and the emergence of the New Testament record. The truths we therefore believe are the focus of the initial studies. *Therefore*'s later studies focus on what believers are therefore called to do, in response to what we believe, based on Who we believe.

Translations and capitalization problem: Verse references are from the NIV translation, unless otherwise stated. Like most versions of the Bible, the NIV does not capitalize pronouns for deity, yet it seems fitting for the human author of these studies to capitalize them. Therefore when the author writes, caps are used, but when the Bible is quoted, they do not appear.

Appendix: Since *Therefore* is covering a broad swath, the Appendix is meant to augment and inform about issues the reader may want to explore more fully. Some full-page entries are from former studies by the same author. The reading lists supply background for what may seem like "sweeping statements" in *Therefore*. Material about the Messianic Movement is included to help familiarize Gentile believers with that very important happening in our times.

Let us join together in Apostle Paul's prayer:

> *For this reason, ever since I heard about your trust in the Lord Yeshua and your love for all God's people, I have not stopped giving thanks for you. In my prayers I keep asking the God of our Lord Yeshua the Messiah, the glorious Father, to give you a spirit of wisdom and revelation, so that you will have full knowledge of him. I pray that he give light to the eyes of your hearts, so that you will understand the hope to which he has called you, what rich glories there are in the inheritance he has promised to his people, and how surpassingly great is his power in us who trust in him.*
>
> Ephesians 1:15-19a (CJB)

Study 1

The Significance of the Packed Word "Therefore"

Welcome to *Therefore!* What a peculiar name for a study. *Therefore* is the third in a series preceded by *All* and *In*. Having studied the others is not necessary for getting into this third one. *(Appendix D summarizes them.)*

All is a summary title for a study based on all that Jesus fulfilled, arising out of the Old Testament. On the road to Emmaus, the night after His resurrection, He opened the Scriptures to two travelers (and thereby also to us) by revealing an amazing fact. Luke 24:25-27 records His disclosure:

> He said to them, "How foolish you are, and how slow of heart to believe all that the prophets have spoken. Did not the Christ have to suffer these things and then enter his glory?" And beginning with Moses and all the Prophets, he explained to them what was said in all the Scriptures concerning himself.

In is a summary title for a study based on all Jesus imparts to all who are in our Lord Jesus, called "the Christ"—derived in English for how Greek would word it or "the Messiah" in Hebrew terms. "In" seems to be such a tiny and incidental preposition, and yet in Scripture, "in" is one of the most important disclosures in God's Biblical revelation. For instance, how significant is the "in" found in these statements?

I Corithians 15:22 "For as *in* Adam all die, so *in* Christ all will be made alive…"

Ephesians 1:7 "*In* him we have redemption through his blood…."

Colossians 1:27 "Christ *in* you, the hope of glory…."

Summarizing the three in short form: Jesus revealed that the Old Testament was *All* about Himself. The New Testament reveals His enabling presence living *In* the believer. *Therefore* our lives are to be lived out in accordance with these marvelous realities.

The word's implications: "Therefore" is God's signal word, meaning "because of this, then that."   It's a cause and effect statement, indicating "because of that, then this." It's a connecting statement, signifying that "because of what has just been said, this is the resulting conclusion, condition, command, or response." How skillfully the Spirit of God teaches us as He helps us grasp "the whole counsel of God," rather than bits and pieces!

The meaning of "therefore" can be expressed in similar ways, too. A shorter and less noticeable synonym is "so," and longer synonyms are "consequently," "since then," and "for this reason." (Various translations may interchange these words.)   Each of these terms lead us to think backward and forward. Each calls us to engage our minds, and hopefully our hearts, with the depth of the truths being revealed. For example, when Hebrews 12 starts out with, "Therefore, since we are surrounded by such a great cloud of witnesses..." we are pointed backward to the whole of chapter 11, on the one hand, but forward to the consider the race in which we ourselves are engaged.

 Try some examples of this "therefore" principle, by examining the backward consideration and the forward urging of these passages. For example, take I Thessalonians 4:18: "Therefore ... encourage each other with these words." (This statement looks back to the promises in 4:13-17, and looks forward to His return, telling us to encourage each other.)

Finish the words of each verse below, and then underneath it, jot down a key word that looks backward for a reason, and a key word looking forward to an indicated purpose.

Hebrews 10:35 "So...

Romans 5:18 "Consequently...

Ephesians 3:14 "For this reason…

Colossians 3:1 "Since then…

THREE PRINCIPLES THAT UNDERGIRD THESE STUDIES

First, please note that the author's firm presupposition is that the Word of God is our sure source, and our totally reliable guide to all truth, and to the true life God wants to impart to us. From man's side, solid scholarship stands behind this assurance, considering the monumental number of Bible manuscripts that are available throughout history, testifying to the reliability of the original text from which our English Bibles are derived. From God's side, we have His testimony to His Word.

Write down exactly what the Spirit says in II Timothy 3:16:

Lest we take for granted our un-matched privilege of having the Scriptures available to us, we should seriously consider the lengths to which our forebearers have gone, in life and death, to transfer God's message to the world. Luke, John, Paul, and others suffered to get their link in the chain of revelation to us. So then, what is a testimony you remember about someone throughout history who has paid heavily to get the Word to the world? Thank God for them!

Write down their name, place, and time in history.

The Enemy of God works tirelessly to separate hearers from the Word of God. In His parable in Luke 8, Jesus warned about Satan's work to snatch the "seed" of God's Word away quickly, lest it grow and produce fruit. Bible study is meant to move hearers to obedience, which can then lead to fruitfulness.

Second, a vital illustration will be repeatedly referred to in this *Therefore* study. We could call it "Three men walking on a wall," and we are indebted to Watchman Nee, a Chinese believer who shared it in *The Normal Christian Life*. ("Normal" meaning not the sub-normal we often settle for.)

> Three men are walking along a wall. One is named FACT, the next FAITH, and the last, FEELING. When FEELING looks all around, he soon falls off the wall. If FAITH keeps his eyes on FACT, FEELINGS soon come along safely behind.

Is the picture clear? This study is intended to encourage us all to keep walking along the wall, with our eyes fixed on Jesus. "Therefore-sensitivity" is a precaution against the Enemy's devices. Satan nudges us to look around at the raging waters, taking our eyes off of Jesus. Our doubt—our loss of the faith link—plunges us into the abyss. Constantly we need to focus our FAITH on the FACT of Jesus' sufficiency, and see our experience eventually follow safely along. "Therefore-sensitivity" is a method for keeping our eyes (FAITH) on the FACTS (what the Word stated before). That done, we are then enabled (BY FAITH) to put into practice (EXPERIENCE/FEELINGS) whatever the FACTS should consequently lead to.

How would you draw the "3 men" illustration? Try it here:

Third, be aware that this study is based on an overall orientation to Scripture which we might call thinking "panoramically." There are many kinds of Bible studies available to us. Devotional studies, for instance, often center on applications to be gathered from one word, or story, or parable. We can profit by many varieties of studies. *All, In,* and *Therefore* are focused on the overall story of God's interactions with humanity, leading to His goal. Pantheistic or atheistic religions tend to project a cyclic interpretation of history. The Judeo-Christian Scriptures interpret history as having a beginning, middle, and an end—that is, they give clues about how God is moving toward His goal. The goal involves His *glory*—a clue word to take note of throughout the Scriptures. How He is proceeding toward His goal is mysterious, yet He gave us clues and revelations. Paul put this wonderfully at the close of the book of Romans:

> *Now to him who is able to establish you by my gospel and the proc-lamation of Jesus Christ, according to the revelation of the mys-tery hidden for long ages past, but now revealed and made known through the prophetic writings by the command of the eternal God, so that all nations might believe and obey him—to the only wise God be glory forever through Jesus Christ! Amen.*

 Thankfully, the Old and New Testaments tell us about the beginning, some of the middle, and point to the end of history. Our generation may actually be coming close to the finish line, at which time our Creator God will accomplish His goal. God's Enemy does not want us to be aware, to care, or to consider these matters. He works to keep us distracted, asleep, and oblivious to the battle for our souls in which the world is engaged—and in which each of us is engaged, whether we know it so or not. In Matthew 24 and 25 Jesus gave clues to the struggle the world would experience when drawing close to God's intervention. He wants us to be awake! "Therefore keep watch, because you do not know on what day your LORD will come (Matthew 24:42)."

♥ *And me?*

How willing am I to commit to examining the facts, engaging my faith, and conforming my life experience in response, by God's grace?

OUR PRAYER:

Dear Lord, May this study serve to focus us on the foundational FACT God has given us (the identity of Jesus), awaken our FAITH in Him, and prepare us to live intentionally and obediently for Him in our daily EXPERIENCE. May we be better equipped for our spiritual battle, at "such a time as this." May we be encouraged to identify with Him in the pursuit of God's goal. May we take heart in light of the marvelous future our Lord so wonderfully promises to those who love Him. In Jesus' Name, Amen.

Ω

Note: Each of the twelve Therefore studies closes with a key verse that is valuable to internalize and hopefully to memorize. See Appendix E for all twelve compiled on one page.

THEREFORE SPEAK

It is written, "I believe; therefore I have spoken." With that spirit of faith we also believe and therefore speak, because we know that the one who raised the Lord Jesus from the dead will also raise us with Jesus and present us with you in his presence. All this is for your benefit, so that the grace that is reaching more and more people may cause thanksgiving to overflow to the glory of God.

II Corinthians 4:13-15

Study 2

The Ultimate Motivation for "Therefore" Responses

Introduction: This is a dangerous study to undertake, because it requires decision. And once the basic decision of life is made, life involvements follow. None of the "therefores" focused upon in these studies are embraceable, unless the ultimate cause for them is settled. They all turn upon one decision, the identity of Jesus. His ultimate question put to those around Him was, "Who do you say that I am?"

Many books talk about spiritual issues, but only one book in the world claims to record what God says about Himself. He revealed Himself through what He told the prophets to say, and then He revealed Himself by sending His Son into the world in human form. We call that thirty-three year visit, "the Incarnation." The Incarnation is the ultimate fact we are faced with, to accept or reject. Did God actually enter history in human form? Was Jesus truly Who He claimed to be? Our answer either causes us to dismiss Him from our lives, or else respond to Him in cooperation with whatever "therefores" flow from His invasion into our world, and the goal toward which He is working.

All humanity, and each of us, has a desperate problem. In the clamor of our writhing world, and in quietness of our hearts, we can hardly deny that humanity is in serious trouble, and we ourselves are without inner peace, unless our relationship with God is settled. We have the privilege of examining the Scriptures God has wonderfully provided to speak to our universal and individual need. We are lost in a forest of trees, and need His viewpoint, from above. We are caught in Time. He speaks from Eternity.

We are advised not to have false expectations if we believe. The Scriptures record Man's long history of rejecting the Creator, from Eden onward. When the Savior was sent, the majority rejected Him. Thereafter in history, the majority has rejected Him. If we accept Him, we will be entering into life through a narrow gate (Matthew 7:13), with a minority of "seeds" that take root among weeds (Matthew 13:37-39). We can expect to be rejected, as He was (John 15:18-25). We will have to live with troubles (John 16:33) and we can count on being in a spiritual battle our whole lives, until Eternity. Counting the cost of following Jesus is sobering. However, counting the cost of rejecting Him, if He truly is who He claimed to be, is even more sobering. Therefore it is wise to make our choice extremely seriously, not based on hearsay or the mood of the times, but based on solid facts.

This investigation takes an historical approach. The Scriptures tell us that God's plan for our deliverance was initiated through a particularly chosen community, through whom the Deliverer would eventually come. Abraham, Isaac, and Jacob's family was chosen for this, and the Exodus was the initial breakthrough that launched God's plan of salvation. Thereafter, the Israelites went through many periods of faithless wandering in their BC centuries. Then the Incarnation broke through, with what only God in the Person of His Son could do: defeat sin and death. Centuries after, Christendom has also wandered unfaithfully throughout our AD period. We find ourselves facing the same choices that men and women have been facing throughout history. We are waiting for God's promised next move.

Therefore proceeds panoramically over major milestones of revelation. To ground our search in history, Jesus' name at the time of the Incarnation will be used to help us remember that the Incarnation was happening in real time, in a real place, among a Hebrew people. *Yeshua* (meaning "salvation") was the Name given to Him by the angel God sent to Mary (Luke 1:31) and then to Joseph: "You are to give him the name Jesus, because he will save his people from their sins" (Matthew 1:21). What English translates "Jesus" was heard as *"Yeshua"* in the language of Israel in the 1st Century. Note that not until the Gospel moved into Gentile territory, among Greek speaking peoples, did the name "Christ" come into use, the Greek term for "Messiah." In English, when we refer to Jesus Christ, it appears to be a first and last name, but it should be understood as Jesus "<u>the</u> Christ"—"the Messiah"—"the anointed one." *(This text will sometimes use "Yeshua" especially when referring to a context during our Jewish Lord's Incarnation, and "Jesus" or "Christ" in the context of the later and wider believing world.)*

Who did *Yeshua* claim to be? That is the question we all have to answer. What are some of the clues that help us answer accurately? The following questions will help us find the clues.

The day of His resurrection, who did Jesus say the Law and the Prophets (i.e. the Old Testament) was about?

      Luke 24:25-27

(See Appendix A, B and C for visuals summarizing some of the main foreshadowings of the coming Messiah concealed in the Old Testament, and revealed in the New.)

When a seeker called Him "good teacher," did He accept the man's estimation of His identity? Notice *Yeshua's* subtle indication of His true identity.

      Matthew 19:16-22

Who did He reveal Himself to be, to the woman at the well? Notice the commonly held expectation of her times.

      John 4: 24-26

Yeshua claimed God's Name! Realize that to use the words "I AM" was to identify with God's name for Himself, given to Moses (Exodus 3:13-15). It is in continuous present tense—as only the Eternal One could be. As He spoke of Himself, what astounding identities did He claim?

      John 6:35

      John 8:12

John 10:11, 14

John 14:6

The climax of Jesus' rejection: As He argued with the Pharisees, what claim most enraged them? If not true, would their reaction be reasonable? There are only two possibilities, true or false, and no one else had ever made such a claim.

What all did Yeshua claim for Himself in the encounter reported in John 8:48-59?

The Gospels provide a living record of people's reactions to the identity claims of *Yeshua.* Many clues stand out to be noticed:

As He did miraculous things, what were these "signs" to accomplish in those who witnessed them?
John 10:30-38

John 14: 9-11

When He quizzed the Disciples as He approached the Cross, with what identity was He satisfied that they had comprehended?
Luke 9:18-22

As He prayed to the Father the night of His arrest, where was He going, and where did He want His followers to go?

    John 17:1-13, 24-26

The Apostle John had walked the dusty earth with Jesus for three years. Who did John recognize Jesus to be?

    John 1:1-3, 14

After the risen Lord's ascension to Heaven, the Epistles were written. Who did the Spirit of God identify *Yeshua* to be in those writings?

    Philippians 2:5-11

    Colossians 1:15-20

The Resurrection was/is the crowning evidence for the identity of the Messiah. It was their insistence on the reality of the Messiah's resurrection that put the early believers at odds with authorities. Peter had seen His glory at the Transfiguration and had witnessed His presence for 40 days after the Resurrection, and Paul had met Him later on the road to Damascus. For examples, examine these next passages:

THE ULTIMATE MOTIVATION FOR "THEREFORE"   21

II Peter 1:16-21 (later in Peter's life)

Acts 13:26-38 (Paul speaking at Pisidian Antioch)

I Corinthians 15:12-19
(Paul reflecting on the Resurrection's necessity)

<u>Believe or reject?</u> Jesus' miracles helped people, but their main purpose was to prove His identity. John tells us that "Even after Jesus had performed so many signs in their presence, they still would not believe in Him" (John 12:37). We today have the Scriptures that record those signs, yet most people do not engage with Jesus. His many miracles—even the greatest one, the Resurrection—all flow out of God's having sent His son into the world. Write down word for word exactly why He was sent.

John 3:16-17

Everyone's choice today: Everything we must choose to believe or reject (or ignore, which amounts to rejection) about Him turns around the question of the *identity* of the One who became Incarnate in our world. His entry, His work, His vindication, His victory, and His goal are all authenticated based upon His identity.

Those who decide to join the Kingdom of God have an amazing future. It will be challenging and difficult, but marvelously rewarding.   If we say "Yes!" to the Father and the Son (the Sender and the Sent), then we start thinking in terms of Who we are called to trust, what we are to believe, and what "therefores" we are called to act upon, to live out, "until He comes" (I Corinthians 11:26).

When He returned to Heaven, He gave His community an assignment, and promised to return the second time to bring His goal to completion. These are the things we will examine in the *Therefore* studies.

♥ *And as for me?*
God gives me choice. Have I made the most important choice of my life?

Prayer:

Dear God, help my unbelief. I need your Spirit's work in my mind and heart and will to carry through with my decision and to live out its implications.

Ω

*Note: As we internalize these key verses, we should consider them in relationship to their contexts. What FACT precedes, to which the "therefore" is responding?

THEREFORE GOD EXALTED

Therefore God exalted him to the highest place and gave him the name that is above every name, that at the name of Jesus every knee should bow, in heaven and on earth and under the earth, and every tongue confess that Jesus Christ is Lord, to the glory of God the Father.

Philippians 2:9-11

Study 3

"Therefore" Facts for All, Jewish or Not

Introduction: The Bible is God's revelation to mankind, both to the people He chose for bringing forth the Messiah, and the rest—that is, the Gentile branches of mankind. The New Testament letters are His message of redemption in terms that speak to both the Jewish and Gentile mind and background. The Apostle Paul's letter to the Romans is a beautiful example of this message to both communities. He keeps making the distinction between them, and speaks to the necessities for each to grasp. He essentially levels the ground in front of the Cross on which Jesus died for *all*. In the meantime, Paul wanted the core of Jewish believers in Rome and Gentiles freshly out of paganism to understand their common guilt and common means of salvation that they both shared, as do we in our century.

Only a few in today's world are privileged to have a Biblical background that informs their understanding of God's wonderful provision for salvation, while the majority of humanity does not. Paul feels a great burden for everyone "without hope and without God in the world," as he describes their condition in Ephesians 2:12. The Spirit of God can stir that passion in our hearts as well.

What calling motivates Paul, and in what order?

>   Romans 1:1-7

>   Romans 1:14-16

Paul's astounding revelation. From the onset, Paul wants to convince both Jews and Gentiles to perceive and believe the amazing good news that righteousness before God does not come from performance, but by *faith*. The Jewish community had long misunderstood this principle, relying on their good works. The Gentiles (in this case, pagan Romans) would have been used to trying to win their gods' favor by their own doings, as well. The baseline of all Paul is saying in this letter is firmly placed on the one truth affirmed in Romans 1:17: "The righteous will live by faith." He will spell out what that truth really means meticulously. The letter to the Romans gives us the rare blessing of overhearing this foundational truth, whether our ears are Biblically initiated or uninitiated. God's Scriptures show how the basis of the salvation that all people need was true even back in Abraham's time 2,000 years before the Incarnation. The same principle was true in Jesus' century, and true thereafter, which includes us. However, this principle of "right standing before God only by faith" is hard to swallow, for both the religious and the irreligious. It strikes a blow to human pride, and is completely foreign to the way people almost anywhere think. So Paul has to start from the beginning and put the spotlight on man's most basic problem. Bluntly put, our problem is our universal captivity to sin, with the inability to resolve our guilt.

The guilt of sin and the inevitability of death confront every person.

> Romans 5:12-19. Where did sin and death come from, and who has overcome them?

What judgment from God does humanity's universal debt of sin rightly result in, and why? Paul makes his case in these first chapters of Romans, before explaining God's mercy—His offer of forgiveness. Going back to creation, he traces man's rejection of God.

> Romans 1:18-2:10. Why are those who reject God guilty, and what kind of living reveals their heart condition?

> Romans 1:24 and 26. Notice what *therefore* God did.

Romans 2:12-3:8. Is the Jew who for salvation depends on keeping the Law of Moses exempt from God's wrath?

Romans 3:9-20. Who does God consider "righteous" and who stands condemned before Him?

To put it succinctly, Romans 3:23 warns every human, and each of us, about our desperate problem. Write it down in bold letters:

Only God could solve every man's and woman's problem. God Himself has provided a solution! We need to firmly grasp the fact of God's own way of solving our problem, for this truth is the indispensable key to salvation for every person.

Romans 3:21-31. How does God say that "righteousness" (right standing before God) is made possible? In other words, how can any sinner be made acceptable to a holy God, anytime, anywhere?

In terms of our picture of the "three men walking on the wall" referred to in Study 1, what is the overarching fact we are to grasp from Romans 4:21-5:2 and then believe, and therefore experience?

Try drawing the three stick men, and label them with a key phrase for the FACT that the man called FAITH must keep his eye upon, for EXPERIENCE to rightly fall in line.

Jesus pointed to *faith* as the key to God's acceptance. John 6:28-29 tells the story: They asked him, "What must we do to do the works God requires?" Jesus answered, "The work of God is this: to believe in the one he has sent."

Paul explained this principle carefully. The New Testament was given by the Spirit of God after Jesus had borne the penalty for our sins on His Cross and had risen from the dead. The Resurrection proved His identity and qualification for this God-sized work for our salvation. The Holy Spirit used Paul to present the whole process of redemption theologically, from creation to the Cross and beyond.

Problem! Trying to please God with good works is a pretty universal approach. Humans are so used to operating on the basis of works—of what they can do to earn acceptance—that to be told they must not do anything, not perform at all, is baffling. It challenges our pride as well.   But our total inability is God's assessment of man. Fallen humans can never truly be holy; we can never pay the debt of sin we owe. In His love, God had to deal with our need Himself, and He chose to do it in the person of His Son. As the Incarnation began, God sent an angel to tell Joseph that "what is conceived in her is from the Holy Spirit. She will give birth to a son, and you are to give him the name *Yeshua* because he will save his people from their sins" (Matthew 1:21a, 22). *Yeshua* means "salvation." The Messiah's openness to all sorts of people as He embarked on His ministry looked very strange to the Jewish leadership. They asked why He ate with "sinners." Jesus answered, "Go and learn what this means: 'I desire mercy, not sacrifice' (Matthew 9:13). For I have not come to call the righteous, but sinners." His enemies performed the religious sacrifices at the Temple day by day, but they did not recognize their own sin and lack of true righteousness before God.

How about us? Let's beware! We who have the Scriptures today correspond to the religious leadership to whom Jesus spoke. We may be blind to our own sin, and may actually be trying to win God's favor by some kind of good works ourselves.

List a few ways you can find traces of that attitude in yourself:

Why did the principle of salvation only *by faith* apply both to observant Jews and to uninitiated Gentiles as well? Notice how important it is that Abraham's experience of faith in 2000 BC preceded the giving of the Law of Moses in about 1400 BC. Abraham is the "father of the faith" for both Jews and Gentiles. Although the whole human race stands condemned, in God's mercy we all are offered redemption in Christ Jesus.

Romans 4:1-21. How was righteousness only by faith demonstrated by the Patriarch Abraham?

Romans 4:22-25. What kind of righteousness does God accept? Whose righteousness is it?

What is the marvel of "imputed" righteousness? It is crucial to understand that the only kind of righteousness that is acceptable to God is an undeserved gift mercifully *credited* to the person of faith. "Credited" is a banking term for an exact transaction. The Savior paid for the sins of the world, and therefore God can declare our sin debt paid. "Imputing" righteousness is something God chooses to do, not something we can do. We can only believe Him in order to activate this amazing transaction. Forgiveness is nothing we deserve, but it is a free gift of God's grace to those who trust in the redemption Christ Jesus has accomplished for us. An amazing summary of this marvelous mystery is stated in just one verse, II Corinthians 5:21. Write it down in bold letters:

Therefore, what are the wonderful out-workings of imputed righteousness? Consider the amazing results for the believer brought about by being credited with Christ's righteousness!

Write down what God credits to His believers and therefore means for us to accept by faith, as explained in Romans 5:1-11:

♥ *And me?*

Therefore, considering these truths, where do I find myself to be in my inescapable condition of desperate need, but also being given the assurance that rescue is not only possible, but deeply desired by the One who made me?

Prayer:

Help me Lord, to grasp and appropriate for myself the amazing revelation of truth as the Apostle John summarized it in John 3:16, 17 (CJB): "For God so loved the world that he gave his only and unique Son, so that everyone who trusts in him may have eternal life, instead of being utterly destroyed. For God did not send the Son into the world to judge the world, but rather so that through him, the world might be saved."

Ω

THEREFORE THE PROMISE GUARANTEED

Therefore, the promise comes by faith, so that it may be by grace and may be guaranteed to all Abraham's offspring—not only to those who are of the law but also to those who are of the faith of Abraham. He is the father of us all.

Romans 4:16

Study 4

Enter the Holy Spirit, and Therefore the "In" Reality

Introduction: Once we have grasped the jolting seriousness of our situation and have thanked God for the deliverance only He could provide, we are tempted to go into default mode and just do what humans always do, try hard to succeed at this new life. We must now enter into His way of living *through* us, by supplying the presence and power of the Holy Spirit, the third member of the Trinity who constitute one God.

Continuity: In Study 3 based on Romans, we focused upon the Scripture's insistence that we could do nothing to pay our own penalty for sin and accomplish our own salvation. We had to admit our need and simply receive God's provision for us in the Savior sent to redeem us out of our lost condition. In this Study 4, we discover that the same principle applies to living the life of faith. We do nothing but cooperate with what God in the Person of the Holy Spirit does IN us.

After the Incarnation, God was about to send another marvelous provision for His people's need. John's Gospel tells us that Jesus proclaimed this coming outpouring of His Spirit at the Feast of Tabernacles in Jerusalem. At a breathless moment during the water-pouring ceremony, Jesus called out: "If anyone is thirsty, let him come to me and drink. Whoever believes in me, as the Scripture has said, streams of living water will flow from within him." In the next verse, John 7:39, John explains, "By this he meant the Spirit, whom those who believed in him were later to receive. Up to that time the Spirit had not been given, since Jesus had not yet been glorified." Well, when would Jesus be glorified? We'll soon find that answer.

Jesus prepared His disciples for a new kind of life in His absence—His life *within* them. The night before His arrest, He talked with them at length. Those precious final revelations are recorded in John 13-17. His men were frightened by His insistence that He was about to leave them, and He was explaining to them how His presence was going to continue to be with them, in a mysterious way. Reading through their whole last consultation together in John 13-17 is best. But for our study's constraints, we will examine highlights about the new relationship with the third member of the Trinity that was about to begin. As *Yeshua* taught during His Incarnation, where did He say the Spirit's presence was, in relation to them at that time, before His exaltation? Where after the Spirit was poured out?

John 7:37-39 states an important clue.

John 14:15-17 announces the change.

What are other names for *Yeshua's* replacement, and Who would the Holy Spirit magnify?
John 15:26-27

What was to be the ministry of the Spirit?
John 16:13-15

How and when was this to happen? *Yeshua's* disciples were left hanging in despair after their Lord's crucifixion, and then were amazed at His resurrection, even though He had repeatedly told them to expect this, as heard in Matthew 16:21, 17:9, and Mark 8:31. He remained on earth meeting with them for forty days, and He gave them a strange command: "Do not leave Jerusalem but wait for the gift my Father promised, which you have heard me speak about. For John baptized with water, but in a few days you will be baptized with the Holy Spirit." (See Acts 1:1-7) They waited and wondered. The Feast of Pentecost arrived, bringing to the Temple a host of pilgrims again—many of whom had been a part of their Lord's crucifixion only fifty days before. Imagine *Yeshua's* community's fear and tension!

On the day of Pentecost, when the Spirit fell upon the believers, Peter was given God's message to explain what was actually happening.

> What had happened in Heaven to cause the Spirit's outpouring on earth?
> Acts 2:32, 33

This pouring out of the Spirit was accompanied with miraculous manifestations of God's presence: wind, fire, unlearned languages, hearing ears, and a new power in Peter, who had recently denied he even knew *Yeshua*. God timed it at the ideal occasion for spreading the glorification of the Son to the known world, because pilgrims had come from many nations to the annual Feast of Pentecost. Something absolutely new was happening.

> What shocked the Jewish community who were present?
> Acts 2:1-12

> Imagine yourself there that day, and record some of your reactions to Peter's bold message.
> Acts 2:14-24

What did David have to do with Jesus?
    Acts 2:25-36

What did the Spirit do that day, and soon thereafter?
    Acts 2:40-47

What was this new form of connection with Jesus going to involve? This is important to us today, because this has been how believers connect with their Lord throughout history, ever since that unique Pentecost. Let's look at a couple of principles:

Who is the source of any fruitfulness, and whose "work" is it? How important is the word "in"?
    John 15:1-5

Notice that fruit in a believer's life is not called really his/her own, but is identified as "the fruit of the Spirit."
    Galatians 5:22-23

Notice that the gifts believers receive are not called their own, but they are identified in I Corinthians 12 as the "gifts of the Spirit" to the whole body of Christ. Who determines who gets what gift?

I Corinthians 12:11

Yeshua explained to the disciples that it was better that He go and the Spirit come. Think why. Unlike Jesus, the Spirit would not be confined to one human body and one generation. He would be able to be with everyone at the same time, and throughout time. He would move from being "with" a believer occasionally (as in Old Testament times), to being "in"—"indwelling"—the believer perpetually.

What new dynamic does His presence make available to believers?

Acts 1:8

How the believers experienced this new relationship with the Lord through the Spirit is evident in Paul's prayer in Ephesians 3:16-21. Write down his phrases related to "power."

<u>Notice the **"Christ"** in the term "in Christ."</u> Why isn't this translated "in *Yeshua"*? After the Gospel spread out over Asia Minor and Greece, the disciples were working among Greek-speaking people. "Christ" comes from the Greek word they used, and it means "the Anointed One"—"the Messiah." In the New Testament, all the Letters except Hebrews were written to congregations in Greek-speaking areas, so the writers used the word "Christ." We would be wise to think "in Messiah" when we see "in Christ." *(See Appendix D's visual, and Appendix E's verses, related to "in.")*

<u>Be awake to the **"in,"** in the term "in Christ."</u> Watch that small word "in," because it has huge implications. Why? Because according to God's Word to us after Pentecost (in the Letters to the young churches), everything that comes to the believer is not because of something we do, but it is ours because we are "in Christ." The power resident in us, the fruit of the Spirit, the gifts of the Spirit, and our blessed future—all of these are ours because of our UNION with Christ. The wonder of God's love INCLUDES us in His love for the Son. We are gathered into the Trinity. That is how *Yeshua's* prayer in John 17 is answered!

> For what does *Yeshua* passionately pray as He faces the Cross and
> His return to "the glory I had with you before the world began"?
> (John 17:5).
>   John 17:20-26

What does it mean to be "indwelt" and "included" in Christ? Let's trace some of God's teachings about this presence and union. What do these marvelous realities accomplish for the believer? Discover from these passages:

Romans 6:1-10

Ephesians 1:13-14

Ephesians 2:5-6

Colossians 1:17-20

Colossians 2:2-3

Colossians 2:9-13

In summary, we are completely dependent upon the Holy Spirit's **indwelling** presence in us, and His **including** baptism of us into the body of Christ—for everything our Lord is working to accomplish through our salvation, and the salvation of the world.   What a surprise, challenge, equipping, and blessing!

Where does "therefore" come in?   The picture of "three men walking on a wall" was introduced earlier: Fact, Faith, Feelings. The Holy Spirit states some of the "in" Facts we trust by Faith, that assist our Feelings (experiences) to rightly follow. God's explanation of our relationship with the Spirit is the Truth we "therefore" believe, have faith in, and live accordingly. Without accepting the truth of our human inability to live the Christian life, we could well struggle a lifetime to produce fruit in our own strength, on a disconnected vine, to use our Lord's analogy (John 15:1-5).

Mystery!   Although he longed for his own people's salvation, the Apostle Paul was assigned to reveal the mystery of God's world-wide plan of salvation to the unnatural branches, the Gentiles. He summarized his calling when writing to the Colossian church:

> "I have become its servant by the commission God gave me to present to you the word of God in its fullness—the mystery that has been kept hidden for ages and generations, but is now disclosed to the saints. To them God has chosen to make known among the Gentiles the glorious riches of this mystery, which is Christ in you, the hope of glory."
>
> Colossians 2:25-27

What is the *mystery*?

♥ *And me?*

What about my own relationship with the Holy Spirit? Am I trying to live a Christian life by my own resources, in my own strength?

Have I believed God and relaxed into His Spirit's keeping, trusting in His power and presence? Ever? At this time in my life?

Prayer:

Lord, I'm so human, and I so want to be in control. Help me believe what You say is the truth of my situation "in Christ." Help me take joy in Your provision of power, and rest in the sufficiency of Your indwelling Spirit's presence. Help me to rejoice because of being "included," according to Ephesians 1:13, 14:

"And you also were included in Christ when you heard the word of truth, the gospel of your salvation. Having believed, you were marked in him with a seal, the promised Holy Spirit, who is a deposit guaranteeing our inheritance until the redemption of those who are God's possession—to the praise of his glory."

Ω

THEREFORE REMEMBER FORMERLY

Therefore, remember that formerly you who were Gentiles by birth and called "uncircumcised" by those who call themselves "the circumcision" (that done in the body by the hands of men)—remember that at that time you were separate from Christ, excluded from citizenship in Israel, and foreigners to the covenants of the promise, without hope and without God in the world. But now in Christ Jesus you who once were far away have been brought near through the blood of Christ.

Ephesians 2:11-13

Study 5

"Therefores" After Yeshua's Fulfillment of the Old Covenant

Introduction: Can we imagine the difficult position in which Jewish believers in *Yeshua* found themselves during the forty years between the Lord's Incarnation and the destruction of the Temple—between the 30s and 70s AD? Imagine being constantly at risk of violence from occupying Romans who had crucified your Lord. Imagine the situation for the 5,000 plus Jewish believers (Acts 2:41, 4:4) who had accepted *Yeshua* as God's true Messiah, surrounded by the majority of their neighbors who followed the Sanhedrin's rejection of His claims. The priests are sacrificing lambs daily at the Temple, yet Messianic believers know that *Yeshua* was the final and perfect Lamb of God, as John the Baptist had announced Him (John 1:29). Study 4 focused upon the arrival of the Holy Spirit at that unique Pentecost recorded in Acts 2. For a few other glimpses of this period of transition from BC to AD realities, look at these accounts:

> The Gospel's proclamation after the healing of the crippled beggar in the Temple.
>> Acts 3:11-26

> The clash with the Sanhedrin over proclaiming the resurrection.
>> Acts 4:1-21

> The arrest, angelic deliverance, and further conflict with the Sanhedrin.
>> Acts 5:17-41

Stephan's defense (Acts 6:8-7:53), stoning, and the great persecution that scattered the church.
Acts 7:54 – 8:4

Connections: Under the circumstances of the spiritual battle they were engaged in, the Hebrew believers needed encouragement and grounding. The Spirit of God used the Letter to the Hebrews to awaken the original Messianic community to the amazing fulfillments of God's purposes that had been "previewed" in the Old Testament. Hebrews provides a densely packed abbreviated summary of various Old Testament "shadows" (Hebrews 10:1) which gave way to "reality" in the fulfillments of the Messiah. *(See Appendices A through C for examples.)* Without the letter to the Hebrews, New Testament believers would be much poorer, for these Scriptures disclose the wider picture of how God went about redeeming humanity. They give us a panorama of history and a depth of meaning of which today's New Testament-focused believers might be oblivious.

Broad sweep: We find more "therefores" in Hebrews than in any other New Testament letter. Why? Probably because the Hebrews had so much background for their faith, that they therefore were superbly responsible to stay faithful to the LORD their God. The chosen people who lived during and shortly after the Incarnation were immersed in the Old Testament. Their Scriptures informed them about human history: creation, the calling of Abraham, his progeny's twelve tribes, their Exodus from Egypt, the Law *(Torah)*, the Tabernacle, the Feasts of Israel, Israel's wilderness wanderings, the conquest of the Land, the Davidic Kingship, the building of the Temple in Jerusalem, the United and Divided Kingdoms' history, the Northern Kingdom's exile and the Southern Kingdom's Babylonian captivity, the Jewish exiles' return, the building of the Second Temple, and the Roman occupation in which they now lived.

Their privilege! Jewish believers who had all this Scriptural background had also witnessed the arrival of the long-expected Messiah Himself. They had seen, or were informed about, His crucifixion and His resurrection.

Furthermore, they were living after the initial pouring out of the Spirit upon the believers at Shavuot/Pentecost, and were themselves indwelt by the Holy Spirit of God. No generation had ever been so informed, so blessed, or so responsible for holding fast to the unfolding of God's whole redemptive plan. They were the community to whom God's mystery throughout the ages was revealed. Paul summarizes it at the end of Romans:

> Now to him who is able to establish you by my gospel and the proc-lamation of Jesus Christ, according to the revelation of the mys-tery hidden for long ages past, but now revealed and made known through the prophetic writings by the command of the eternal God, so that all nations might believe and obey him—to the only wise God be glory forever through Jesus Christ! Amen.

Paul explained this newly discovered mystery to searching Gentiles. They could accept it at face value. Jewish believers, however, had to re-consider how Gentiles fit into their practice of separation. The Letter to the Hebrews draws the two Covenants together, disclosing layer after layer of the newly revealed mystery of the Messiah's identity and goals. It fits their community with new glasses.   It gives the believing remnant of Jewish believers a whole new understanding of the age-long purpose of their Covenant, Law, Priesthood, Sacrifices, Tabernacle, Feasts, and Messianic hope.

Parenthesis: Our privilege!   Today we have the complete canon of Old and New Testament Scripture, which allows us, whether Jew or Gentile, to be informed about God's panoramic plan of redemption. The mystery of the Messiah is the Old and New Testament's inseparable disclosure. The Letter to the Hebrews gives us the profound privilege of looking over the shoulders of Hebrew believers as they first read this new message to them. Christians in western nations have tended to interpret the Bible with a Gentile mindset. The Letter to the Hebrews helps us read the Scriptures through Jewish eyes, in the context of their religious and cultural background. This is a tremendous gift. It gives us a short course in how God's chosen people were practicing many aspects of the Mosaic Covenant at the time of the Incarnation. In the sacrificial Lamb of God, and in our Lord's ministry as our eternal Great High Priest, the Old Testament practices found their fulfillment. This document reveals layer after layer of valuable insights that can deepen our grasp of God's truth and help us face our own call to faithfulness.

Hebrews is probably the most dense New Testament letter. It is based upon the intricate ceremonial Law and practice taught throughout the books of Exodus, Leviticus, Numbers, and Deuteronomy in Israel's *Torah*. God had told His people to make the Tabernacle "exact, according to the pattern" (Exodus 25:9, 40) because each imbedded element would point to the Messiah, and would "speak volumes" when He would eventually arrive.

As an example, consider this *Torah*-informed passage in Hebrews 10:19-22:

> *Therefore brothers, since we have confidence to enter the Most Holy Place by the blood of Jesus, by a new and living way opened for us through the curtain, that is, his body, and since we have a great priest over the house of God, let us draw near to God with a sincere heart in full assurance of Faith.*

What aspects of Temple worship stand out in these verses?

What do these Hebrew Old Covenant worship practices reveal? To grasp the profound meanings of Israel's worship, Gentiles needed to learn that the Most Holy Place is where the Ark of the Covenant stood in the heart of the Tabernacle. They (and perhaps we) needed to learn that the Great High Priest once a year placed the blood of Atonement on the cover of the Ark. We need to realize that the curtain separating the Holy Place from the Most Holy Place was torn open at the moment of the Messiah's death for humanity's sins (Luke 23:45). The body prepared for Jesus (Hebrew 10:5) was torn open, figuratively opening up a living (not animals dying) way. Having the Old and New Testament, we can correlate both stages in the story of redemption, moving from the earthly Tabernacle (Exodus 25:8) to the eternal Sanctuary in Heaven (Hebrews 8:5, 9:23-26). As we meditate on such profound mysteries, we must depend on the Holy Spirit, Who was sent to be our Teacher about these things (John 16:13, 14). *(See Appendix B and C on the Tabernacle and Feasts.)*

Searching through Hebrews for venerated elements of the earlier Covenant, we see how *Yeshua* is presented as their fulfillment. The Messiah is the mediator of the new and better covenant that was prophesied to come (Jeremiah 31:31-34, and referred to in Hebrews 8:7-13).

> The New Covenant is based on the superiority of the Son.   What words or phrases describe Him in Hebrews 1:1-3?

Consider the cascading "better" elements that *Yeshua's* arrival actualized. Why is the Messiah's everything "better"?

> Why a better High Priest? Hebrews 4:14-5:10; 7:26-28

> Why a better priesthood? Hebrews 5:6-10; 7:1-28

> Why a better covenant? Hebrews 7:21-22; 8:6-13; 9:15

> Why better blood? Hebrews 9:11-14

> Why a better sacrifice? Hebrews 10:12-14

Why a better hope? Hebrews 7:19; 10:23

Therefore, certain *responses* are recommended:

In light of our sinless Priest's sympathy, therefore...
Hebrews 4:14

In light of our Great High Priest's ministry in the true Holy of Holies,
therefore....
Hebrews 10:19-25

In light of the lives of the faithful "cloud of witnesses," therefore...
Hebrews 12:1-2

Therefore, since _____, let us
_____
Hebrews 12:28

In light of the Lamb's final sacrifice having been made, "therefore"
what?
Hebrews 13:15

This priceless message meets ongoing generations' need to grasp the "betters" of the Incarnation. The Old Covenant recorded clues for recognizing the work and identity of the Messiah, whenever He would come. These early "types" help believers more deeply realize what all *Yeshua* fulfilled. The sacrificial system practiced at the Tabernacle and Temple was visible and tangible, whereas their fulfillments are spiritual, invisible, and must be taken on faith. The 1st Century community was tempted to revert to Temple Judaism—to the physical, to the accepted, to traditions that did not require faith in the unseen majesty of the Messiah seated at God's right hand. Furthermore, unknown to them, the Temple would be gone in a few decades. Gentiles would have little opportunity to explore these practices except for the description of them in the Old Testament Scriptures, and interpreted for the whole Church in the book of Hebrews.

Therefore, let us deeply value what Hebrews can do for us today.

> ➢ Hebrews firmly places the Incarnation in the center of redemption history, unifying it (Chapter 1).

> ➢ Hebrews speaks to faltering and suffering believers (Chapters 2-4, 6, 10, 12).

> ➢ Hebrews gives the reader valuable warnings (Chapters 3-6).

> ➢ Hebrews offers us a valuable summary of the worship practices God gave to Israel (Chapters 5, 7-10).

> ➢ Hebrews calls the people of God to faithfulness (Chapters 10 through 13).

To summarize, Hebrews' "shadows" and "realities" (Hebrews 8:5; 10:1) disclose a priceless goldmine of meanings behind these venerable practices. The book of Hebrews assumes the readers' familiarity with these ceremonies which they had been commanded to practice perpetually.

Note: Spending an extra session on the patterns of the Tabernacle and Feasts in Appendixes A through C could be rewarding.

♥ *And me?*

In what ways has Hebrews deepened my understanding of who Jesus is?

What foreshadowings make me appreciate Him in a fuller way? (See the Appendixes to consider the many foreshadow meanings.)

Prayer:

Thank you, Father, for the Church's Hebrew forebears. May we value Your uniquely chosen people. For as Paul prayed, "Theirs is the adoption as sons; theirs is the divine glory, the covenants, the receiving of the Law, the Temple worship and the promises. Theirs are the patriarchs, and from them is traced the human ancestry of Christ, who is God over all, forever praised! Amen." Romans 9:3b-5

Ω

THEREFORE LET US DRAW NEAR

Therefore brothers, since we have confidence to enter the Most Holy Place by the blood of Jesus, by a new and living way opened for us through the curtain, that is, his body, and since we have a great priest over the house of God, let us draw near to God with a sincere heart in full assurance of faith.

Hebrews 10:19-22a

Study 6

Why the Spirit Led the Root to Therefore Accept Branches

Introduction: We would not be studying the Word of God today, if it had not been for the decisions of the "Jerusalem Council" reported in Acts 15. Those decisions inaugurated a whole new trajectory for the chosen people's knowledge of *Yahweh*. How did the message of *Yeshua,* a crucified and resurrected man in Jerusalem two millennia ago, escape the confines of Israel?   The Book of Acts tells the fascinating story of how God unveiled His mysterious plan for reaching the whole world.

Continuity: Study 5 focused on the Letter to the Hebrews' presentation of the Messiah's fulfillment of the sacrificial pattern of worship which was so deeply imbedded in Hebrew culture. Study 6 will turn now to the situation that arose when Gentiles began accepting Jesus as the Savior of the whole world. Suddenly, the original Messianic Jewish community was faced with an unexpected relational and theological crisis. The book of Acts records their experience as they sought the Holy Spirit's guidance.

What happened to His thousands of disciples after Jesus' ascension? Acts 2 records the shocking events of the Day of Pentecost, not two months after *Yeshua* had been crucified, and had come forth from the grave. How awesome it must have been for the Levitical priests at the Temple to have discovered the curtain veiling the Holy of Holies to have been torn open at the moment of *Yeshua's* death. Up to that year, the ancient records of God's dealings with His chosen people had focused primarily upon the Israelites - Abraham, Isaac, and Jacob's family—through whom the Messiah was to be born.   How shocked that community was fifty days after *Yeshua's* sacrifice, when at the Feast of Pentecost the Spirit of God fell upon people from all sorts of nations.   That once-in-history outpouring announced the Son's enthronement in Heaven! (Acts 2:33).

From then on, Acts records one surprising experience after another for the Disciples. Often they were by specific divine appointments, such as Phillip's in Samaria and then with the Ethiopian official (Acts 8), Saul's meeting the risen *Yeshua* on the road to Damascus (Acts 9) and becoming Paul, and Peter's experience with the Roman household of Cornelius (Acts 10, 11). Some Jewish believers began objecting to Peter's fraternization with unclean Gentiles, so he reported how the Spirit had fallen on Gentiles in Cornelius' household in the same way He had fallen on the Jewish (and proselyte) community in Jerusalem at Pentecost.

> What was Peter's conclusion about God's will?
> Acts 11:15-17

Jesus' proclamation was beginning to materialize. Acts chapter I reports the crucial last words of the risen Jesus before He ascended to Heaven.

> What had *Yeshua* told them would happen, and in what order?
> Acts 1:7-8.

God had the whole world in His mind and heart. His intention to make redemption available to the whole world through the Son whom He had sent was beginning to take visible shape! Persecution was fanning the Messianic community out into Judea and Samaria, and eventually into Gentile territories, such as a city north of Israel named Antioch. Messianic believers there (Jewish and Gentiles) sent Paul and Barnabas out further into Asia, in the area we now call Turkey. Gentiles in city after city embraced *Yeshua* as their Savior. Paul's first trip into Asia is related in Acts 13 and 14, a roller coaster of reaching, teaching, receiving, being rejected, being stoned, returning, strengthening new believers, and reporting back to the sending body in Antioch.

To the synagogue at Pisidian Antioch in Asia, (not the Antioch from which Paul was sent, on the Mediterranean) Paul spoke powerfully to Jews and Gentile "God-fearers" in a synagogue.

After tracing Hebrew history from Egypt to David, on what did Paul base his insistence on salvation being available to Gentiles?

Acts 13:23-41

Write the conclusion about God's inclusiveness in Paul's "therefore" stated in Acts 13:38-39:

But back in Jerusalem: Hearing about all this Gentile response, some of the Jewish leaders in Jerusalem demanded these Gentile converts be circumcised, the rite that would make them acceptable as "Jewish." Disagreeing deeply, Paul and Barnabas went to Jerusalem to settle this sensitive matter, and so the "Jerusalem Council" reported in Acts 15 was convened.

Had the Jerusalem Council's decision sided with the Pharisee-led argument, the prophesied (Isaiah 49:6) "light to the Gentiles" would have been extinguished. Converting Gentiles to Judaism would have had little chance of being multiplied the world over. Converting Gentiles to Yeshua, who they began calling "Christ," was happening in spite of any brakes being put on, because God the Holy Spirit was guiding the process.

This amazing development: The door of faith opening to the Gentiles (Acts 14:27) was directed by the Holy Spirit. Notice the leadership of His quiet and unseen presence being attributed to the Holy Spirit in Acts 13:2, 4, 52; 15:8, 28. Had it been left to the early believers, the Good News would probably have been reserved for the Jewish community. It took God's intervention to turn them outward. Their confusion between viewpoints came to a head when they called the conference in Jerusalem.

The Jerusalem Council's deliberations changed the world. Reading Acts 15 carefully, let us follow the two sides' viewpoints.

> How did the Judaizing party reason?
>> Acts 15:1, 5

> How was salvation possible in Peter's eyes?
>> Acts 15:7-11

Peter's reference in Acts 15:8 is based on God's surprise to him in the home of Cornelius (told in Acts 10) and summarized in his explanation to Jewish believers in Acts 11. We need to lay aside today's disputes over varying viewpoints about "speaking in tongues" and focus on the original miraculous pouring out of understandable languages foreign to the speakers on the day of Pentecost. A similar baptism with the Holy Spirit was repeated in Cornelius' Gentile home, as Peter reported in Acts 11:15-17.

> What was God communicating through this evidence of the Holy Spirit's presence?

God had commissioned Peter as the first of *Yeshua's* disciples to reach out to Gentiles (Acts 15:7) and Paul, at his conversion, was chosen to carry on from there (Acts 9:15).

> What was Paul's and Barnabas' report to the conference?
>> Acts 15:12

What did James realize was happening?
Acts 15:13-14

On what Old Testament Scriptures did James base his thinking?
Acts 15:15-18

What was James' final conclusion?
Acts 15:19-21

To whom did James attribute the decision?
Acts 15:28

The Council's crucial and history-changing ruling was that the Holy Spirit had shown that circumcision was not deemed necessary for Gentile believers. It had been a covenantal sign between God and His chosen people, but keeping the Law was not the basis for salvation, as the Jewish teachers of the day were mistakenly assuming. What did the Messiah's followers insist was the only basis for their salvation, any Jew's, and any Gentile's?

Write down this rock-solid fact in which we believers today put our own faith.
Acts 15:11

What practical step did the Council take then, to put their decision into action?
   Acts 15:22-29

We need to understand the reason for the Council's sparse but important requirements of the Gentile believers (Acts 15:23-29). Why these? If they were to become "one man" (Galatians 2:14, 15) with Jewish believers, they would be fellowshipping together, and that would surely include eating together. Thus respect for Jewish dietary restrictions would be important. (Acts 6:1-6 gives us a food-based picture of conflicts that were already being dealt with between Grecian and Hebraic Jews.) More important would be complete separation from idolatry, which included eating "meat sacrificed to idols." Sexual immorality was a regular practice in pagan rituals and practice. Practicing sexual purity would be a challenge for Gentile converts, but God had commanded it in His original Ten Commandments (Exodus 20:14) and faithfulness in marriage was one of the hallmarks of true believers' spiritual health and witness then, as it is today.

How did the Jerusalem Council's decisions work out in the first century? Acts gives us a play by play account. We need the Letter to the Romans for insight into the mystery of God's workings in the mix of Jews and Gentiles, theologically. So to Romans 9-11 we will go in Study 7.

How did these two, no, three communities interact between the first and twentieth centuries? We must go to history for that answer, and we need to realize and be honest about the facts. The two millennia from Abraham through the Israelites' Exodus deliverance, wilderness wanderings, and experiences in the Land were rife with rebellion, unbelief, and idolatry. Only a remnant (Isaiah 10:21-22, Romans 11:5) stayed faithful. Christendom's two millennia since the Incarnation bear similar marks of the great Deceiver's successes. Yet there is still the remnant, and God's victory is ultimately assured. We will follow the thread of His unchanging purpose in the next few studies, culminating in His magnificent goal.

♥ What about me, today?

As a Jew or a Gentile, have I realized the significance of the Spirit's direction that history-changing Jerusalem Council day a few years after the Incarnation? How has that trajectory affected me personally?

Prayer:

Oh dear Father, thank You for your unfailing purpose that included me! Help me to realize what you are working toward. May your Spirit work within me to want to join with You, and with all those who pledge their lives to You as their Savior and Sovereign.

Ω

THEREFORE JUSTIFIED

Therefore, my brothers, I want you to know that through Jesus the forgiveness of sins is proclaimed to you. Through him everyone who believes is justified from everything you could not be justified from by the Law of Moses.

Acts 13:38-39

Study 7

Why Jewish/Gentile Disunity Therefore Developed

Introduction: God's intervention into history in the Incarnation radically upended the Jewish community. Thousands of the common people received Jesus as their promised Messiah, but the majority followed the Sanhedrin's leadership, and rejected Him. Two Jewish communities emerged, the believing Messianic Jews (who the Spirit eventually led to accept believing Gentiles), and the unbelieving traditional Jews (who did not). The new faith community had to face this challenging Jewish separation at the same time God was requiring their acceptance of "unclean Gentiles" into their midst. No wonder the Spirit of God had surprising things to teach them.

Background: History's saga reveals a checkered story of relational struggles between Messianic believing Jews and unbelieving Jews, as well as both of their struggles at the hands of Gentiles. Today we inherit the sins of the past. Worldwide Christians should count the Messianic community as our faith's "founders." Furthermore, believers today need to be aware of God's heart for the other community, the larger Jewish majority who reject Jesus. Paul poured out his heart about God's ache over the lost condition of Israel. They were God's chosen people—His covenant people, yet they rejected the Son whom the Father sent to fulfill their Scriptures. "He came to that which was his own, but his own did not receive him" (John 1:11). The promised "seed of Eve" and "seed of Abraham" had been prophesied to bless the whole world (Genesis 3:15; 12:3), yet He was rejected when He arrived. His work of redemption was good news for Gentiles who believed, as Paul expressed in Galatians 3:26-29. Today it is finally received as good news for Messianic Jews, Israelites who accept *Yeshua's* fulfillment. But they still ache over their unbelieving relatives. Added to their leadership's original rejection of Jesus in the 1st Century, the Jewish community today is deeply alienated from the Cross by the myriad of tragic relationships that have developed between Jewish people and Christendom over the centuries, culminating in the Holocaust.

Continuity: Study 4, based on the Book of Acts, recounted the New Covenant's widening out to potentially include the whole world. Paul then was led to explain the Spirit's surprising inclusion of Gentiles from a theological viewpoint. This necessary and timely information for the Body of Christ today is primarily available to us in Romans and Galatians, the focus of Study 6. Study 7 now looks at what went wrong.

We in the "West" owe our being reached with the Gospel largely to the Spirit's ministry through the Apostle Paul. Although thoroughly Jewish, Paul was commissioned by God as the Apostle to the Gentiles (Acts 9:15, Galatians 1:16; 2:7-9). Acts summarizes the matching historical situation with the letters written over these crucial years. Paul yearned over his flocks of Gentile believers, as demonstrated in his letters to the young churches in Asia and Macedonia. The Galatian letter demonstrates Paul's pastoral care over a congregation troubled by "Judaizers"—those who believed that practices of the Old Testament were binding on Gentile converts, especially circumcision.

The life-defining question of the Letter to the Galatians: "How can any Jew or Gentile be justified before God?" Justification is an accounting term. Galatians 3:6 speaks of justification being "credited" by faith. "Credited" refers to a payment—in this case, the substitutional sacrifice by the Savior for the world's sins, including our own. Being "justified" (by faith in the sin payment of the Lamb of God) is how God made it possible for a sinner to be put back into restored relationship with Him.

Write down Paul's summary of this crucial fact of the faith, word for word:
   Galatians 2:15-16

The concept of "salvation by faith" (being made righteous before God, accepted into life eternal) is a blow to human pride. The Jewish community had been keeping the Law of Moses for generations, and they had drifted into thinking their keeping it, i.e. their works, saved them from God's judgment. All along, God's purpose in the sacrifices had been to remind His people that sin brings forth death—death of the sinner, or else of a substitute. In His mercy, God had allowed animal substitutes in the sacrifices of the Tabernacle and Temple. These practices foreshadowed the sinless Lamb's sacrifice, the only one that could completely pay for the sins of the world (John 1:29, Isaiah 53). Jesus fulfilled the Old Covenant through His death and resurrection. He introduced the New Covenant the night before He went to the Cross.

Write down the clear statement of Galatians 2:21 word for word here:

"But, but...," they may have argued. Jewish people traced their heritage and calling to the patriarch Abraham, who lived 2000 years before Christ. So Paul dealt directly with God's purpose revealed to Abraham on the basis of promise, not law (Galatians 3:15-18).

On what basis was Abraham "justified"?
Galatians 3:6-9

And what was God's goal in which He allowed Abraham to share?
Galatians 3:8, 14

The "seed of Abraham" can be thought of in two ways. Who is the promised singular Seed? Who are also included in Him "corporately" as co-heirs with the Seed?
Galatians 3:15-16, 19

Galatians 3:26-29

Jewish and Gentile believers were to be a "corporate" faith community. Romans chapters 9 through 11 explain crucial facts to the New Covenant community. These are greatly needed facts for the times in which we live. Great pressures and persecutions are falling on Jewish people worldwide, and especially on the state of Israel. Are Gentile believers not to identify with God's heart for His covenant people—those who gave us the Scriptures, and our Savior? Singularly, Jesus was "the root out of Jesse" (King David's father) according to Romans 15:12, and calls Himself "the root of David" in Revelation 5:5 and 22:16. "The root" is also a corporate term for the cultivated olive tree (Israel) into which wild branches (Gentiles) have been grafted. "Boasting against the root" (Romans 11:18), the sin of Christendom, has born bitter fruit over the centuries, and is festering menacingly today.

Romans 9 to 11 unfolds right "root and branch" relationships. This instruction was written to a mixed congregation of Jews and Gentiles. The early believers were struggling then to understand their mysterious situation, and we need serious enlightenment on it today.

Why could seeking Gentiles, instead of traditional Israelites, obtain righteousness?
Romans 9:30-32

What did Israel fail to grasp, in spite of zeal?
Romans 10:1, 3

How is justification really obtained?
Romans 10:8-13

What was to be the mysterious role of Gentile belief, in regard to Israel?
Romans 11:11-15

How did God ordain the order of the New Covenant community's root and branch relationships?
Romans 11:16-24

What is the purpose of the "hardening" mystery?
Romans 11:25-29

What two brands of sinners can receive God's mercy?
    Romans 11:30-32

What was Paul's final advice to the Messiah's mixed community?
    Romans 15:5-13

Deviation! Sadly, within a few decades the Gentile branch began to boast over the Jewish root, birthing tragic enmity throughout AD history. Even First Century documents show Gentile Christian patriarchs beginning to ostracize Jewishness. In Constantine's time, the power of Rome forbade Sabbath-keeping and altered the Feast holidays. The bowling ball of "replacement theology" was launched down the long lane of history, slowly veering into a shameful gutter. Claiming that the Church had replaced Israel as God's chosen people, Christendom began to consider Jewish "chosen-ness" finished. This presupposition led to Gentile attitudes that for Jewish people spelled deep suffering: restrictions, repressions, persecutions, exiles, pogroms, and sometimes attempted genocide. *(See Appendix F for sources documenting these historical facts.)*

Admitting the sins of Christendom: This breakdown of unity forged by the Jerusalem Council of Acts 15 needs to be understood by its inheritors—many of today's Christian denominations. World conditions are forcing thinking people to review history and come to terms with long-standing false positions which have led to injustices instigated by Gentiles and suffered by Jewish people throughout the last 2000 years.

Heavy casualties caused by whom? Unrecognized spiritual warfare has been decimating Christendom on many battlefields. Participants have often been unaware of being combatants in the on-going war of the ancient Serpent against God and His people (Revelation 12:17). The Deceiver has been crafty in pitting God's faith communities against each other.

Yeshua's rejection: Gentiles sometimes ask, "Why, of all people, don't Jewish people accept their well-documented Jewish Savior?" Let's review history. Jewish expectations of the coming Messiah were more physical than spiritual. They wanted a king who would deliver Israel from Rome at the moment. Jesus' Kingdom was as wide as the world, and eternal. Jewish leaders were envious of Jesus (Matthew 27:18, Mark 15:20, Acts 7:9; 13:45; 17:5). Israelites inherited their leaders' unbelief and their cover-up of the Resurrection (Matthew 28:11-15). Furthermore, Christendom's treatment of Jewish people since the First Century has deepened their disdain for all things "Christian"—things symbolized by Jesus and the Cross. All Jewish people (both those who accepted and those who rejected Jesus) have shared two things: their ethnic roots, and having to live under prejudice the world over. Humanity's resentment of God and His "chosen people" is tell-tale evidence of widespread cooperation with "the god of this world"—Satan (I Corinthians 4:4).

Today's bad news: Is the "grafted-in branch," the Church, willing to face the two-thousand year record of sins against their "root"? Few people today are aware of horrific Gentile history with the Jewish people. This is a time of reckoning. Today's world is inheriting the consequence of these faith-communities' sins. Resulting conflicts threaten on every hand—anti-Semitism plus anti-religion (especially the Christian religion)—throughout the world. Western civilization, once based on Scripture, appears to be sliding mindlessly down a slope into apostasy, immorality, and idolatry. Founded as Judeo-Christian nations, today's materialistic "West" makes little place for God, religion, or "special people." In the face of spiritual unfaithfulness on many levels, militant Islam is profiting mightily.

This is a day for restoration! As the world turns further away from our Creator, those who love God need to come together. This is a time begging for unity, a unity whose decimation awaits being realized, admitted, confessed, and forgiven, in preparation for restoration of relationships.

> At this time of reckoning, what "therefore" might Gentile believers be warned about by Romans 11:17-24?

Today's good news: In spite of ominous clouds on the horizon, one heartening sign is also appearing. The natural olive tree is budding! After two thousand years, Israel became a state in 1948—a political favor related to the guilt of "Christian" Germany's Holocaust. Amazingly, in the 1960s in America, the "Jesus people" movement in California included many Jewish believers. Meanwhile in Israel, the Spirit of God began bringing many to believe that their Messiah truly was, and is, *Yeshua.* David H. Stern in Israel in 1988 published *The Messianic Manifesto* calling Messianic believers to insist that Jewish people can rightfully be 100% Messianic and 100% Jewish at the same time. He also published *Restoring the Jewishness of the Gospel* to awaken the Church to this serious departure. *(David Stern's books are listed along with others in Appendix F.)*

Setting the scene: These stirrings morphed into Messianic congregations across America, Israel, and the wider world. Ample evidence shows that the tide of Jewish acknowledgment of their Messiah is turning. This "budding of the olive tree" is one expected sign of "the last days." Israel's coming increasingly under attack is another.   That eventuality leads us into the considerations of Study 9, focused on warfare and suffering.

❤ *What about me?*

Am I aware of Christendom's treatment of Jewish people, and its result? Do I see evidences of this tragedy?

If not, would I be willing to expose myself to some of the documentation recommended in Appendix F?

Prayer

We praise God for His love for all nations, along with Paul's conclusion of Romans:

Now to Him who is able to establish you by my gospel and the proclamation of Jesus Christ, according to the revelation of the mystery hidden for long ages past, but now revealed and made known through the prophetic writings by the command of the eternal God, so that all nations might believe and obey Him—to the only wise God be glory forever through Jesus Christ. Amen.

Ω

THEREFORE CONSIDER

Consider therefore the kindness and sternness of God: sternness to those who fell, but kindness to you, provided that you continue in his kindness. Otherwise, you also will be cut off. And if they do not persist in unbelief, they will be grafted in, for God is able to graft them in again.

Romans 11:22-23

Study 8

We are Therefore the Messiah's Ambassadors

Introduction: Once we've received new life in Christ the Messiah, we depend upon His sufficiency, not our own. Thereafter He has work for us to do. "For we are God's workmanship, created in Christ Jesus to do good works, which God prepared in advance for us to do" (Ephesians 2:10). We each look for how He wants to work through us. One of the ways will involve reaching out to those who have yet to know Him.

Passion to redeem people begins in the heart of God. As we begin to bond with Him, we develop a concern for those around us, and for people we don't even know who have not heard about the forgiveness and love of God.

> Yeshua was sent to earth for this very reason. What did He say?
> Matthew 20:28

After redeeming us at the cost of His own blood, He deployed His disciples to carry that Good News forward as He departed to the Father.

> Put yourself among those present, and hear Yeshua speak:
> Matthew 28:16-20

He didn't send them out in their own strength—which was weakness—but empowered by the Holy Spirit He would send.
Luke 24:45-49

Acts 1:8

A royal assignment: When persecution eventually scattered the believers out of Jerusalem, the Spirit gave Peter and Paul specific assignments. Both were Jewish, but Paul's assignment from the Lord was to reach Gentiles (Acts 9:15, Galatians 2:2). That meant going to foreign cultures. It was like becoming an ambassador. Ambassadorship implies going from one country to another, and that was what was happening as the Gospel spread beyond Israel. The Messianic Kingdom, however, was not defined geographically. His is an eternal Kingdom.

Meet Corinth: The 18th chapter of Acts tells us how Paul got into relationship with the largely Gentile community at Corinth in the area we call Greece. It was a Roman colony, full of pagan god worship, with a generally Gentile population along with a small diaspora Jewish community living there. The time frame was just a couple decades after Jesus rose from the grave. Paul reached the Corinthian seekers on his second missionary journey.

Meet Paul: Genuine believers in our Lord Jesus Christ will one day meet the Apostle Paul. In the meantime we come to know him through his writings, for next to David, perhaps no other Biblical writer reveals more of his heart to us than Paul. Reading his letters to the Corinthian community with the Spirit's help, we can sense something of the loving relationship he had with those he had introduced to the Lord there. It is the kind of love we may feel for our children, for those dearest to our own hearts. He saw those He brought to Jesus as his children and as brothers and sisters in the faith.

The book of Acts records how their relationship started. According to Acts 18:18, Paul (joined by Silas and Timothy) had spent a long time in Greece in the area of Achaia and Corinth, where he first met Priscilla and Aquila, Titius Justus, Crispus, Sosthenes, and many Gentiles who became first-generation believers. Later, Paul wrote letters back to them, and mentioned making a third visit. Messages were not simple to send in those days, and we are highly blessed to be able to see these letters centuries later.

Paul's emotions are palpable as expressed in II Corinthians. There had been a problem there, and a rebuke and a response for which the letter called 1st Corinthians is the background. His love for this community comes through strongly in his next letter. He speaks of his heart or their hearts repeatedly in II Corinthians, in verses 3:3; 4:6, 16; 5:6, 10; 6:11, 13; 7:3.

II Corinthians 7:3 summarizes his heartfelt commitment: "You have such a place in our hearts that we would live or die with you"—(the believers in Corinth and Achaia, II Corinthians 1:2). Paul had come close to dying repeatedly, as he shared in chapter 6. Today's believers in many areas of our world are also living close to death all the time. This precious Biblical passage is one that they experience deeply. More comfortable Christians may need to be steadied by our suffering brothers and sisters' faithfulness as shadows deepen in our own lap of witness to Jesus in our generation.

Connecting with Paul's progression: Having dealt in II Corinthians with the disciplinary problem that occasioned the earlier letter, Paul goes on to pour out his overarching passion—his sense of being compelled to get the truth of salvation in the Lord Jesus to both Gentile and Jewish seekers. He builds his case step by step, from the Letter's third through the fifth chapters. We can recognize in them that Fact/Faith/Experience formula with which we are familiar: "Since this is the Truth, and I believe it, therefore I live it out." With many "therefores" throughout a few paragraphs of his letter, Paul keeps connecting the progression of his thinking. His argument should be taken as a whole. It is helpful to read II Corinthians 3:7 to 5:21 as a unit, trying to hold Paul's deep connections together in our minds and hearts. Read the passage through at one sitting. Then read it again, considering these questions:

What two glories is Paul contrasting?

II Corinthians 3:7-11

Therefore what?

II Corinthians 3:12-18

Therefore what further, about "glory"?

II Corinthians 4:1-6

Along with this glory, what struggles are also experienced?

II Corinthians 4:7-12

Notice the progression of "Fact, Faith, and Feeling":
    II Corinthians 4:13-18

The believer's suffering may result in what?
    II Corinthians 5:1-10

What is the sure fact that constrains Paul to persuade people?
    II Corinthians 5:10-11

What is the only reasonable progression in II Corinthians 5:14-16?
        The fact:

        The faith:

        The experience:

Therefore what is the supreme truth Paul yearns to tell the world?
  II Corinthians 5:17-19

Therefore what is the believer's calling?
  II Corinthians 5:19-20

How can Jesus' mission of reconciliation be summarized in one profound sentence? What is the "exchange"?
  II Corinthians 5:21

We call this astounding mystery of reconciliation *"imputed"* righteousness. What an amazing exchange we are privileged to proclaim! This imputed righteousness—simply credited in response to faith—has been God's method from Abraham's day forward (Genesis 15:6, Galatians 3:6)!

An ambassador is deputized to carry a message. An ambassador is sent. Our wonderful God sent His Son to earth to accomplish the reconciliation we are now sent to announce. What a privilege to carry the Father's message! We are the "knowers," "believers," and "experiencers" sent to a poor lost world of people who don't know, have no chance to believe, and are hungering for experience they can't receive until they hear the truth to believe. That's the motivation behind Wycliffe Bible Translators, the Jesus Film Project, Missions Perspectives courses, and the like. Each of us is called to be an ambassador commited to implore people somehow, in one way or another.

♥ *Myself?*
In what ways am I fulfilling my "ambassadorship"?

Prayer:

Oh Lord, only Your heart can sufficiently motivate ours. As we go forth as ambassadors, may our oneness with You "speak" the reality we are proclaiming in the spirit Paul expressed in II Corinthians 3:4-5: "Such confidence as this is ours through Christ before God. Not that we are competent in ourselves to claim anything for ourselves, but our competence comes from God. He has made us competent as ministers of a new covenant—not of the letter but of the Spirit, for the letter kills, but the Spirit gives life."

Ω

THEREFORE IMPLORE

We are therefore Christ's ambassadors, as though God were making his appeal through us. We implore you on Christ's behalf: Be reconciled to God.

II Corinthians 5:20

Study 9

Therefore Expect Warfare and Suffering

Introduction: Contrary to the comfortable assumptions of a "modernly devised Jesus," *Yeshua* spoke bluntly about the rejection and tribulation His followers could expect. The night before His betrayal, He warned them, "If the world hates you, keep in mind that it hated me first" (John 15:18). He also assured them that "in this world you will have trouble, but take heart! I have overcome the world" (John 16:33).

Context: All the "therefores" we have tried to respond to in these studies need to be considered in light of the cosmic, contemporary, and personal war we are engaged in, whether we are aware of it or not. *Yeshua* kept warning his followers about the cost of discipleship. Not only did it demand a believer's all, it also came with the promise of many difficulties. His disciples lived out their trust in Him accompanied by suffering and martyrdom. Paul would warn us, "Therefore put on the full armor of God, so that when the day of evil comes, you may be able to stand your ground, and after you have done everything, to stand" (Ephesians 6:13). We trust in God's grace on life's battleground. John Newton's hymn, "Amazing Grace," states it for us: "Through many dangers, trials, and snares, I have already come. T'was grace hath brought me safe thus far, and grace will see me Home."

What did *Yeshua* actually say about the cost of discipleship? Does it match the messages of many a pseudo-Jesus created for today's "easy believe-ism"?

Matthew 16:24-26

Luke 14:25-35

How can a disciple live faithfully in light of *Yeshua's* seemingly impossible assignments? Only He can live out that kind of life, and that is exactly what He does for us as we stay connected to the Vine (John 15:5). We live by the Spirit's presence and power. As we depend on Him, we are also warned to be alert to the deceptive inroads of the world system, the lusts of our flesh, and the wiles of the devil. The Scriptures tell us what our situation really is, and give us multiple examples of how those deceptions have crippled the believing community over the ages.

We don't need to be in the dark about our struggle. When we read the Scriptures panoramically and try to look down from Eternity, we see that the human race is engaged in a cosmic war. We are given enough glimpses of this battle to realize that all the sons and daughters of Adam, including ourselves, are engaged in a battle. Some of the glimpses are found in these passages:

> Who enticed and deceived our first parents?
> Genesis 3:1-15

> How universal is sin and death?
> I Corinthians 15:22

Who was and still is "the dragon" trying to destroy?   Are we
included?

> Revelation 12:1-17

Since the Fall, who did *Yeshua* actually say is the prince of this
world?

> John 12:31, 14:30

With whom and where are spiritual battles actually fought?

> Ephesians 6:10-12

How can the believer be prepared to do spiritual battle? Realizing the peril of
our situation, we must seriously consider the weapons God has provided and
use them. Note that some are defensive protections and some are offensive
weapons.

Draw a stick soldier and label our spiritual weapons:
Ephesians 6:13-18

Old Testament examples of faith: Hebrews chapter 11 gives us an overview of the warfare of Israel's faithful throughout the ages.

What kinds of suffering did the believing community experience?
Hebrews 11:32-40. (Notice both the delivered and undelivered.)

In light of Hebrews chapter 11, therefore... what admonitions are given? (Notice the action words: throw off, run, fix, consider, endure, strengthen, level.)
   Hebrews 12:1-13

New Testament examples of suffering: Our Savior is the prime example of suffering. Jesus warned His followers about being hated. Acts records and the Letters refer to mistreatment.

   Notice that suffering and persecution were taken for granted.
      Philippians 1:29

      II Timothy 3:12

When flogged, what was the Apostles' response?
    Acts 5:40-42

When Stephen was stoned, his response reflected his Lord's heart (Luke 23:34).
    Acts 7:59-60

When flogged and jailed, what was Paul and Silas' response?
    Acts 16:22-25

Peter warns us repeatedly about what all believers—including ourselves— are to expect. Suffering is referred to about 18 times in I Peter. Tradition says Peter himself was crucified. What amazing attitudes and affirmation of blessings are evident in these Scriptures?
    I Peter 1:3-7

I Peter 4:12-16

I Peter 5:6-11

It will be worth it all!   The book of Revelation gives us glimpses of escalating cataclysms at history's climax. In spite of all these realities and warnings, we are to be encouraged by the assurance that all this life's warfare will finally end, and that God's peace will finally reign in splendor.

John was told in Revelation 21:5 to write down a message.
Write down God's promise here, word for word:
Revelation 21:3-4, 6-7

Our Lord warned His people what to expect when His Second Coming was close.

> Do the signs of our times sound like *Yeshua's* description?
> Write down some of the aspects we are to expect:
> Matthew 24:3-35

> What therefore did the Lord counsel, in light of His return?
> Matthew 24:42

Realize the primary focus of the Enemy's warfare. Gentile believers may not be aware of the horrific suffering of God's called-out people. Throughout Biblical times and to this day, they have endured sufferings designed to obliterate them, yet have survived as a people, like no other. God has preserved them over and over again, as His undying love for them promised.

Why all this suffering for the "chosen people"? One reason is related to God's discipline for a long history of their disobedience and idolatry—for breaking their covenant with Him, as warned by Moses (Deuteronomy 26:16-30:20). Secondly, let us not forget that strategically, God's "chosen people" have been the primary target of Satan's attacks and deceptions over the ages. He made desperate attacks on Yeshua, the most Jewish of all Jews,* God's instrument for redeeming mankind. Thirdly, much suffering has originated from men, for human pride results in mankind's deep resentment toward a community known as uniquely "chosen by God." It has not been easy for them to bear His Name.

---

* Because the very essence of being Jewish is being obedient to the *Torah*, God's Law, and Yeshua obeyed it perfectly.

<u>What did Yeshua warn His followers?</u> Quite in contrast to today's false "prosperity gospels," *Yeshua* promised suffering to His first century Jewish community.   As time went on and believing Gentiles were adopted into this "chosen" community of faith in the God of Abraham, Isaac, and Jacob, the Enemy and the world hated them too.

Even early in His ministry, see what He said:
Matthew 5:10-12

What did Yeshua tell His messengers to expect from the world?
John 15:18-25

<u>Satan's tactic against those who love God is to "divide and conquer!"</u>

The Spirit baptized both Jewish and Gentile believers into one body (Ephesians 4:5). They were to become "one new man" in *Yeshua* (Ephesians 2:15). In retaliation, Satan's deceptions have nudged Jews and Christians into adversarial relationships that have caused great suffering over the centuries. Seeds of anti-Semitism were planted in spurious writings of early Church fathers. The decrees of "Christian" emperor Constantine brought severe persecution upon Rome's Jewish population. False positions tend to be passed on and cause havoc over time. The Holocaust did not occur in a vacuum. Study 7 introduced facts about this breakdown of relationships. *(Sources documenting injustices to Jewish people over the centuries are listed in Appendix F.)*

Encouraging signs. Only in recent decades has the Messianic Movement's appearance begun to call forth healing between Jewish and Gentile believers in *Yeshua*. Meanwhile, the world's hatred for Christians as well as for Jewish people appears to be accelerating. This is another signal pointing to the deliverance only the Second Coming of the Messiah can bring.

Is the world's trend upward? Our leaders try to run the world independently of God. Does mankind seem to be making much headway in solving humanity's recurrent struggles with our sins of hate, greed, prejudice, injustice, and the like? Solzhenitsyn will long be remembered for his diagnosis of both Russia's and America's problem: "Men have forgotten God."

Why has the Messiah's return lingered so long? *Yeshua* promised to return a second time, in glory (Matthew 25:31). Why has that not happened yet? What clues do we get from these Scriptures?

Why, from God's standpoint?
II Peter 3:3-13

Might the body of Christ bear some responsibility for the long lag before our Lord's coming?
Matthew 24:14

Have both Old and New Covenant communities been unfaithful? Has the church had her own "wilderness wandering" over the centuries since the Incarnation, somewhat as Israel was untrue to God pre-Incarnation? Are the judgments which God had Jeremiah pronounce on Israel a picture in microcosm of the judgment which the whole world faces in macrocosm? These things bear thought.

Your viewpoint?

As time marches on, we are running our own lap in the race of life. We are one generation closer to the world's judgment and Eternity being issued in. Suffering in today's world is rampant and swirling over the globe. With more Christians having been martyred in our century than all previous centuries, these are not "normal" times. Believers want to be among the faithful remnant, but we are warned that faithfulness may be costly. We are tempted to fear as the body of Christ's suffering and persecution creeps closer to our own lives.

We will be wise to prepare. Spiritual preparation is more necessary than physical. Primary are staying close to the Lord, and being nourished by His Word. We learn from other communities of the faithful who have passed through the fires. Suffering believers consistently witness that God undertakes for His own in times of persecution, purifying them, and drawing them close. "The hardest times were often the most blessed in terms of our closeness to the Lord," many affirm.

Our earthly bodies hold God's great treasures in breakable "jars of clay" (II Corinthians 4:7). Writing to the suffering Corinthian believers, the Apostle Paul admits his own weakness and difficulties, having repeatedly faced death. Yet he reminds them of sure resurrection. We can be encouraged by his strengthening affirmation:

> *"Therefore we do not lose heart. Though outwardly we are wasting away, yet inwardly we are being renewed day by day. For our light and momentary troubles are achieving for us an eternal glory that far out-weighs them all. So we fix our eyes not on what is seen, but on what is unseen. For what is seen is temporary, but what is unseen is eternal."*

II Corinthians 4:16-18

And the Spirit assures us of total security:

> *Who shall separate us from the love of Christ? Shall trouble or hardship or persecution or famine or nakedness or danger or sword? As it is written: "For your sake we face death all day long; we are considered as sheep to be slaughtered." No, in all these things we are more than conquerors through him who loved us. For I am convinced that neither death nor life, neither angels nor demons, neither the present nor the future, nor any powers, neither height nor depth, nor anything else in all creation, will be able to separate us from the love of God that is in Christ Jesus our Lord.*

Romans 8:35-39

♥ And myself?

Which equipment of the believer's armor (on my stick figure drawing of Ephesians 6:13-18) am I using? Which am I omitting?

How am I looking at the threat of suffering, and also the promise of glory?

What promises in the Word am I holding fast to? Am I embedding them in my mind and heart—therefore memorizing them perhaps?

Prayer:

Lord, help me to absorb and accept the eventuality of suffering in my own life. Thank you for lifting my sights to the eventual joy and glory, highlighted for us in I Peter 4:12, 13: "Dear friends, do not be surprised at the painful trial you are suffering, as though something strange were happening to you. But rejoice that you participate in the sufferings of Christ, so that you may be overjoyed when his glory is revealed."

Ω

THEREFORE HUMBLE YOURSELVES

Humble yourselves, therefore, under God's mighty hand, that he may lift you up in due time. Cast all your anxiety on him, because he cares for you. Be self-controlled and alert. Your enemy the devil prowls around like a roaring lion looking for someone to devour. Resist him, standing firm in the faith because you know that your brothers throughout the world are undergoing the same kind of sufferings.

I Peter 5:6-9

Study 10

The Sure Expectation of His Coming is Therefore Our Comfort

<u>Introduction</u>: For centuries, Jesus' followers have been crying out "Maranatha"—"Come Lord!" (I Corinthians 16:22). It's what they count on. The cynical call them "pie in the sky by and by" believers. They believe it because they are sure that their Lord does not lie, and that He keeps His promises.

<u>Context</u>: The Bible calls the period after the Incarnation "the latter days." It also speaks to conditions in the last days, as II Timothy 3:1-5 predicts. Every generation since the Fall has had its own manifestations of humanity's sinfulness and strife. Our own is seeing evidence of men's brokenness taken to a higher degree, and a broader spread. The media makes us aware of a veritable plague across the world—hate, revenge, intolerance, scattering, and atrocities. The digital age given over to globalization makes it all the more possible for evil to spread like a cancer, and for diseases of body and mind to infect unsuspecting populations who were once left to themselves. Deep suffering is striking millions. Christians face hostile secularism. Militant Islam is strident. And Israel is at the crux of today's complicated world configuration.

<u>People are crying out, "Is there any hope?"</u> God-sized problems demand God-sized solutions. In His mercy, the Father sent the Son to earth to solve man's humanly-unsolvable need to be reconciled to Him. Our Creator has given the world centuries to accept or reject His Son's work of reconciliation during this "the age of grace." The Scriptures warn us that although His love makes Him wait, His patience will finally come to an end, which is called "the Day." Accounts will have to be examined. Justice will finally have to be done. The Day of Judgment of the world, and of individuals, ultimately will arrive. For those who have embraced the Son of His love, however, there is great hope for future restoration and blessing.

God promises that wars will cease, that peace will come. Scripture assures us that this healing will not come through man's efforts. God will have to step into our broken world. Although Adam's race desperately needs to turn to God in humility and repentance for the mess we've made, no generation seems to have done so. Only when God decides to say "Time!" will the world's wars really cease and enduring peace come.

"How long, Lord?" That's our perpetual question. *Yeshua's* disciples asked it (Matthew 24:3) and we ask it still. It's obvious that the world needs a Deliverer! Thoughtful modern writers have framed this ancient and present need in allegorical form. Are we close to "The Return of the King," as Tolkien's allegory pictures history?

Or is "Aslan on the move?" as C.S. Lewis puts it in his Narnia series? In addition to turbulent world conditions that we focused upon in Study 9, what clues could we glean from today's Christendom? False "gospels," apostasy, and luke-warmness seem rampant in the organized church. On the other hand, as the darkness deepens, the light grows brighter. The faithful remnant is taking the command to reach every tribe and nation very seriously in recent decades. Furthermore, whole new waves of maturing young non-Western churches are engaging in the Lord's commission to reach the world.

What hint did the Lord of the harvest give, about the timing of His return? Matthew 24:14

The "olive tree is beginning to bud," as well. After 2000 years, long scattered Jewish people are constituted as a nation again. Although largely unbelieving, especially after the Holocaust, Israel in the last few decades is seeing a new phenomenon—the rebirth of the Messianic Movement that originated in *Yeshua's* generation. Jewish people who now believe He really was and is the Messiah meet in congregations all over the world today. *The Messianic Times* presently lists over a hundred Messianic congregations in the United States, and app.kehilanews.com/congregations lists dozens in Israel.

<u>Some Gentile Christians are admitting Christendom's long-ignored sins</u> against the Jewish people. Some are beginning to ask for forgiveness and reconciliation. They are realizing that Jewish believers are handicapped in reaching their unbelieving community, due to centuries of mistreatment in "Christian nations." They are beginning to awaken to the crisis of faith caused by the Enemy's having divided and nearly conquered the people of God on the spiritual battlefield. These changes may be harbingers of the Lord's return. Consider these possibilities:

> What if Gentile believers got a feel for Paul's concern for Israel's salvation and his deep appreciation for the Church's Jewish patriarchs? Romans 9:1-5

> How does God see the relationship between Jewish and Gentile believers? Ephesians 2:14-18

> How does Scripture present the mystery of Jewish and Gentile disobedience? Romans 11:25-32

Gentile believers are noticing that God's calendar revealed in the Old Testament Feasts throws light on the historical progression of His plan of restoration. It is obvious that the three Spring Feasts were fulfilled when Jesus *was* the Lamb of God at the Passover; He *was* the unleavened bread; and He *was* the First Fruit from the dead. The arrival of the Holy Spirit at the Feast of Pentecost fulfilled the fourth feast. The last three await fulfillment. This period between the first and second comings of the Messiah to earth appear to be the "summer" of seed-sowing and growth, before the Fall Feasts, the time of harvest. Since the first three were fulfilled in just one weekend during the Messiah's first coming, the last three could well happen quickly, as well, at His second. Those who are watching for His return expect the fifth, sixth, and seventh feasts to be on the horizon. They listen for the Feast of Trumpets' warning (fifth feast) to be ready for the Great High Priest's emergence from the true Tabernacle in Heaven on the Day of Atonement (sixth, actually a fast). They look forward with joy to the last (seventh: code-word, "finished")—the Ingathering of those who have loved God—when salvation's harvest is complete. *(For more on the Old Testament Tabernacle and Feasts, see Appendix A, B, and C.)*

"The Day of reckoning" is another way the closure of the world's saga is presented in the Bible. On that awesome Day, God will wield a double-edged sword—cutting judgment for some, yet blessed deliverance for those who have put themselves in His care. The Prophets spoke often of this Day. Zechariah 12:10-14 predicted Israel's mourning at the return of "the One who they pierced," yet Zechariah 13:1 promises their cleansing.

Yeshua kept teaching about what was yet to come. Sometimes He spoke of the Kingdom of Heaven in parables, and sometimes He made blunt statements. Consider the point of each of His teachings that follow:

> What assurance did *Yeshua* give to the Disciples at their Passover meal the night of His arrest? John 14:1-4

When did He tell them they should realize that "your redemption is drawing near"? Luke 21:5-28

What did He indicate Jerusalem would have to do with His return? Matthew 23:37-39

What would conditions be at the time of His arrival? Matthew 24:4-36

Who knows the timing, and how are we admonished? Matthew 24:36-42

The risen Christ also revealed a panoramic unfolding of the future in the book of Revelation. Its entirety is overwhelming. What are some encouragements in these few passages?

Blessed promises to those within the Church who "overcome":
Revelation 2:7, 17, 26-28; 3:12-13, 21-22

Israel's 144,000 servants of God sealed:
Revelation 7:3-8

"The wedding of the Lamb" and His Bride, the Church:
Revelation 19:6-9

Blessedness of the new Heaven and earth:
Revelation 21:1-4

The Bridegroom's promise to come for the Bride "soon":
    Revelation 22:7, 20

The Apostolic writings: Before the Apocalyptic revelation was given to John, the Disciples were teaching the infant churches and writing Epistles to them in the first few decades after the Resurrection. We can glean some hints about the future from the Apostles' Spirit-informed messages. These clues give us a general overview of this mysterious climax when Time will end, and Eternity will be issued in.

The Rapture:
    I Thessalonians 4:13-18

Christ's second appearance:
    Hebrews 9:28

The believer's inheritance kept safe till God's power is revealed:
    I Peter 1:3-8

God's patience:
    II Peter 3:3-10

Christ's sufferings and the glory that would follow:
    I Peter 1:10-12

The crown for those who "love His appearing":
    II Timothy 4:7

A new Heaven and new earth, the home of righteousness:
    II Peter 3:10-13

"The Day of His coming" is the "blessed hope" (Titus 2:13) for those who have come to love God. "Hope" in this context does not imply uncertainty, but confidence. His community sometimes disagrees over how to interpret the clues given about His return—such as when it will come, and in what stages it will happen, and how it could be "charted" in time. For this study's purposes, the important truth is that IT WILL HAPPEN. The Prince of Peace, the Alpha and Omega, will return. The King of Righteousness will finally reign. The character and the reliability of the Promiser is the basis for our certainty.

How do these disclosures about the future apply to us today? The Day calls forth two responses. When the Disciples spoke of their Lord's return, they said, "Therefore encourage each other with these words" (I Thessalonians 4:18). When they envisioned the end-time judgment coming, Peter asked, "What kind of people ought you to be?" (II Peter 3:11). *Yeshua's* prediction in Luke 21 reveals both responses: "Men will faint from terror, apprehensive of what is coming on the world." Yet to those who love Him, He promised that, "When these things begin to take place, stand up and lift up your heads, because your redemption is drawing near" (Luke 21:28).

♥ *And me?*

As I anticipate the two-fold sword at the climax of history, am I encouraged about His future return and rule, or am I gripped with fear?

Is my relationship with the Judge of all the world settled?

Am I resting in the righteousness He imputes to me on the merits of His Son?

Prayer:

How we thank you, dear Father, for the promise of Your Son's return in glory! Meanwhile, we are encouraged by Paul's prayer in Romans 15:13: "May the God of hope fill you with all joy and peace as you trust in him, so that you may overflow with hope by the power of the Holy Spirit."

$$\Omega$$

THEREFORE ENCOURAGE EACH OTHER

For the Lord himself will come down from heaven, with a loud command, and with the voice of the archangel and with the trumpet call of God, and the dead in Christ will rise first. After that, we who are still alive and are left will be caught up together with them in the clouds to meet the Lord in the air. And so we will be with the Lord forever. Therefore encourage each other with these words.

I Thessalonians 4:16-18

Study 11

The Goal Toward Which All the "Therefores" Have Led

Introduction: To begin with, let's admit that trying to comprehend God's ultimate goal is frankly beyond human conception. As Job realized, "Surely I spoke of things I did not understand, things too wonderful for me to know" (Job 42:3b). This Study 11 focuses on things too wonderful to know. And yet the progressive revelation of redemption announced to us in the Bible shows us that God deeply wants to reveal Himself to His beloved creation. He desires to be known in His entire splendor.

Way down deep, we who He has created are all yearning for something in our lives, something, well, "glorious"—something marvelous, beautiful, warm, radiant, enfolding, and ultimate! God also yearns for us to experience the wonders of His gift of "glory," and to be gathered into its fullness. Let's try to uncover some of the depths of satisfaction promised to those who follow their deepest heart cry to fulfillment.

"Glory" is sprinkled all through the Bible, but since it is such a mysterious concept, the reader can miss it. Keep your eye on *glory* throughout the Scriptures. Highlight it somehow, and linger over it attentively. If we look up the word glory and all its derivatives in a Bible concordance, we find hundreds of references to the meanings and experiences related to God's glory, and ours, to glorying, being glorified, glorious, and such.

God's original creation of *light* seems to be connected to revealing God's glory. God created light (Genesis 1:3). Light enables His glory to be put on display. His created heavens and skies display His glory (Psalm 19:1).

Are His creatures responsible to acknowledge the visible world's Creator?

Romans 1:18-23

 As the story of redemption progresses, the Kingdom of God is central. Glory radiates from the King and the Kingdom of God—an actual Person and a real place.

The Messianic King is called "the king of glory" (Psalm 24:7-10).

The glory of God's Kingdom is extolled in King David's Psalm.
Psalm 145:1, 11-13.

At the birth of the Messianic King, angels announced "Glory to God in the highest." The wise men came searching for the King of the Jews (Matthew 2:2) and that title was even posted on His Cross (Matthew 27:37).

Yeshua's "Lord's Prayer" established the Kingdom as the priority of prayer (Matthew 6:10).

Yeshua's teachings and parables in the synoptic Gospels are full of descriptions of the Kingdom of Heaven. He assured His people, and even Pontius Pilate, that His kingdom was not of this world (John 18:36).

Yet at the climax of history, Heaven cries out, "The kingdom of the world has become the kingdom of our Lord and of his Christ, and he will reign for ever and ever" (Revelation 11:15). Yeshua, the Word of God, the King, is named at the end of Time: "KING OF KINGS AND LORD OF LORDS" (Revelation 19:13, 16).

Repeatedly, His glory appears in the Bible. During the Incarnation, God's glory was made visible to man in *Yeshua* Himself.

Three disciples were privileged to get a glimpse of His glory before His post-Resurrection glorification.

Luke 9:28-36

As He was praying the night before the Cross, the Lord earnestly prayed for His disciples to eventually be present with Him, and see what?

John 17:24

How does the writer of Hebrews speak of the glory of the Son? Write out His description in Hebrews 1:3:

Yeshua's many miracles testified to His identity. He made clear the purpose of His last miracle (raising a man from his grave who was four days dead), defeating death itself. Write out His stated purpose, in John 11:4:

When humans behold God's glory in awe, they worship. In Old Covenant times, Moses' face became radiant as he beheld God's glory.

Why did Moses cover His face?
(Exodus 34:29-35)

After the Incarnation, something similar happens to those who focus on the face of Christ. In contrast to the fading glory Moses experienced, the believer's Spirit-sustained glory can be ever increasing.

What is the difference, and who makes that difference?
II Corinthians 3:7-18

How awesome are the GLORY facts of which the Lord has assured us! They are awesome, powerful, and precious. Stop to thank and praise God for them!

Right now for His disciples on earth:

   We are called into His Kingdom and glory. I Thessalonians 2:12, II Thessalonians 2:14

   We are being transformed as we reflect His glory. II Corinthians 3:18

   We glory in His service. Romans 15:17

   His heirs share in His suffering, and in His glory. Romans 8:18

   His glory outweighs our suffering. II Corinthians 4:17, Romans 8:18

   Since God sees eternally from beginning to end, He says the believer is already "glorified" in His eyes. Romans 8:30

At His coming and thereafter:

   Trials will result in glory when Jesus the Christ is revealed. I Peter 1:3-7

   Believers will accompany Him at His appearance in glory. Colossians 3:4

   Seeing people who they have helped come to Jesus is the believer's glory and joy when the Lord Jesus comes. I Thessalonians 2:19, 20

   A crown of glory awaits the faithful. I Peter 5:4

As we have thought through the preceding facts, the splendor of God's intentions for His own is overwhelming. When these amazing truths sink deeply into our souls, they bring forth amazement, awe, thanksgiving, joy, and anticipation. They lead us to worship the One who has loved us so.

***

But wait! Let's refocus. We've been looking at the goal of all the *therefores* from our human standpoint. On the other hand, how does reaching God's goal look from His standpoint? Suppose we move our camera, so to speak, up, up, up to where we are viewing the climax of history from Heaven's perspective.

The book of Revelation is a gift we should not take for granted! God had the Son give it to John for the Churches' encouragement over the ages. Without it, we would have no sure information about the culmination of history. This allegorical panorama moves back and forth from Heaven to earth. Its worship scenes disclose glimpses of an awesome future which we could never imagine unless informed by the Apocalypse. Because of the Revelation, the Church has been blessed to glimpse happenings in Heaven. We are is then able to sing with the angels worshiping at Heaven's throne, "Worthy is the Lamb!" (Revelation 4:11; 5:9, 12).

Revelation Chapter 7's worship scene reveals worship in Heaven, tied to happenings on earth. From Revelation 7:3-17, consider:

What racial group is "sealed"?

What ethnic groups are at the throne?

Who are they worshiping?

What heavenly group is also worshiping God?

What situation did the multitudes come out of?

Why are their robes white?

Therefore, the Lamb will be their_____ and what will the Lamb and God do?

Scenes in Revelation's Chapters 7 and 14 reveal the divine plan coming into fulfillment! If we are aware of God's promises to Israel, and Christ's assignment to the Church, these scenes reveal wonderful fulfillments. The Bible tells one story. Make the connections. God's promise to Abraham in Genesis 12:3 that "all peoples on earth will be blessed through you" is being fulfilled. (This promise is restated in Acts 3:25 and Galatians 3:7-9.) The "all Israel" in Romans 11:25, 26 (all twelve tribes) are present in these scenes. "The ends of the earth" of Acts 1:8 and "the whole world" of Matthew 24:14 are present: "a great multitude that no one could count, from every nation, tribe, and people and language."

The fulfillments appear in the Biblical order – that is "to the Jew first, and also to the Gentile."

Who are the "first fruits" of the blessing? Revelation 14:3-4

To whom else is the Gospel proclaimed?
Revelation 14:6

Revelation's chapter 19 suggests more completions. From the first nine verses, consider why all Heaven is shouting "Hallelujah!"

Has God's promise in Genesis 12:3 been fulfilled?
Revelation 7:9

Has God's judgment on sin (personified allegorically in "the great prostitute," called "Babylon" in chapter 18) finally been meted out?

Has the Lord's Prayer (Matthew 6:9-10) that He taught His disciples to pray been fulfilled?

With what ceremony is the consummation of the love story of the Son and His Bride introduced? (Revelation 19:7)

***

Let's refocus our lens again, shrinking our view down, down, down from Heaven, to earth's future. Revelation 21 portrays God's new creation—a "new Heaven and new earth"—centered around a "new Jerusalem." God and man are dwelling together, their fellowship restored. The old order has passed away. Everything is new. Awesome and magnificent beauty is portrayed. Nations are bringing their glory into His Kingdom. God and the Lamb are its light!

Has *Yeshua's* prayer in John 17:24 been fulfilled?

Revelation 21:3

Has the last of the seven Feasts unto the LORD—the Ingathering—been fulfilled? That is, have the Old Covenant and New Covenant people been gathered together in joy? How is their continuity and unity represented allegorically?

Revelation 21:9-14

Genesis and Revelation were recorded over fourteen centuries apart, but the author of Scripture, the Spirit of God, has been revealing one progressive story. Revelation 22 comes full circle from the tree of life in the Garden of Eden to the tree of life in the New Jerusalem (Revelation 22:2, 14, 19). Here the water of life appears again (Revelation 21:6; 22:2, 17), that water about which *Yeshua* spoke during His Incarnation, in John 4:10, and John 7:38. Has the curse been reversed?

Revelation 21:4

If we take in these truths by faith, we are brought to our knees in gratitude! Yet it is not only the *absence* of death and sin that gladdens our hearts, but the *presence,* the eternal presence, of God's love that this whole story has revealed to us in one way after another: the love of the Father for His children, the love of the Son for His Bride, the love of the Spirit for each one He has been personally indwelling. Amazing, amazing grace! Amazing love!

<u>The magnificent story of redemption</u> closes with a love call that heralds the beginning of a new and eternal future.   A Lover is calling to His beloved. He displays His glorious identity to her (the people of God) in at least six different ways in Revelation 22:12-16. Write them down:

♥   *And my response?*

In the depths of my spirit, how am I responding?

God's goal of my sharing in His GLORY is fulfilled, actually, by my responses. I ask myself, has He become:

➤ My Savior? (I've repented, believed, and received Him.)

➤ My Lord? (I've surrendered my life to Him.)

➤ My King? (I gladly take up citizenship in His Kingdom.)

➤ My Bridegroom? (I revel in His love and await its fulfillment.)

➤ My ultimate hope? (I trust the mysterious and marvelous plan of God for His Own.)?

If my answer is a committed "yes!" to all on that list, then I will be one who will be "with Him, seeing His glory" in answer to His profound prayer that night of His betrayal (John 17:24). Amazingly, I will someday be seated at the Wedding Feast of the Lamb!

What will I be feeling on that day?

Prayer:

Thank You, thank You, Lord Jesus! Wonder of wonders, that all who love You are included—mercifully, graciously, and joyfully included in Your Bride! Help me to give You my full devotion. May Your life in me draw others to You, on earth, and forevermore.

Ω

THEREFORE DO NOT LOSE HEART

Therefore we do not lose heart. Though outwardly we are wasting away, yet inwardly we are being renewed day by day. For our light and momentary troubles are achieving for us an eternal glory that far outweighs them all. So we fix our eyes not on what is seen, but what is unseen. For what is seen is temporal, but what is unseen is eternal.

II Corinthians 4:16-18

Study 12
Therefore in the Meantime...

Introduction: Since all hell seems to be breaking loose over the world these days, the people of God are supposed to be able to interpret the signs of the times. People who remind unbelievers of God in some way are resented. Meanwhile, believers look to Him for guidance and the strength to endure inevitable persecution—to "overcome" as the Scriptures put it. The Book of Revelation gives us a glimpse of believers in Heaven who overcame God's enemy, "the accuser of our brothers." How? "They overcome him by the blood of the Lamb and by the word of their testimony; they did not love their lives so much as to shrink from death" (Revelation 12:11).

Continuity: Study 11 focused on our blessed confidence that God's goal is certain to be achieved. His glory will flourish, and He promises that the believing remnant will be included in the glorious life He has planned. That being assured, we believers find ourselves at this point of history in a world in woeful revolt against our Maker, and foreseeably on the brink of the prophesied Day. This final study 12 focuses on Jesus' followers' need to draw close to our Lord, and take our stand at a time which may cost us our lives. Over the globe in this last century more Christians have been martyred for their faith in Jesus than in all history before. Of course we know that there are worse things than dying. God has strengthened His people repeatedly in previous periods of persecution and suffering, times that seemed to their generation to be close to the end of God's patience. How can our generation of believers be prepared to take our stand faithfully today, when harbingers of God's judgment are multiplying astronomically? And short of dying, how are we to live faithfully in such a time as this?

"Therefore," as Peter asks, "what sort of men ought we to be?" Peter did not have the Book of Revelation since it was given after he was martyred, but he was quite aware of the Day of the Lord. The Old Testament (Peter's Bible) spoke of the Day often. *Yeshua* warned that it would surely come like a thief. Peter had heard the Lord disclose what to expect when the "last days" arrived. Matthew heard *Yeshua* too, and recorded those things in Matthew chapters 24, 25. God has seen to it that we also have these harbingers in His Word 2000 years later.

Peter's letters are timely for us today. Look through his advice found in II
Peter 3:1-18, noticing the main conclusions (italicized):

> Who has been giving Peter's community *understanding*?

> What do *scoffers* do and say?

> What are they *overlooking*?

> What sort of *cataclysm* is predicted at the Day of Judgment?

> How different are the world's and God's *clock*?

> Why does God seem slow in keeping His *promise*?

> When it comes like a *thief*, what will happen to the earth?

> Therefore, what should the believer *do* now?

> What promise encourages *joyful expectation*?

The risen Lord gave the Church a final message, without which we would
know little about the future outcome of God's purposes.   The Lord gave the
apocalyptic vision to John "for the churches" (as most Gentile-generated
translations read), or "for the Messianic communities" (as *The Jewish New
Testament* translates Revelation 3:22).   Taking a slight tangent, remember
that our Study 7 discussed causes for today's Messianic community's sensitive
choice of words. Over the centuries, the term "church" has become associated
with a building, denomination, national designation, or a hierarchy of power.
To unbelieving Jewish people, the word "church" evokes resentment.   The
early meaning of "church," however, was simply a fellowship of believers in a
certain area. The 1st Century church included Jews and Gentiles, all of whom
had accepted *Yeshua* as the Messiah. Chapters 2 and 3 of Revelation record
messages given in around 90 AD to seven churches in Asia Minor, all in the
Gentile territory we call Turkey today.   Some see these letters as messages
to the whole (code word "seven") Church in every century, and some see in
them as the Church's historical chronology from the Incarnation to the end.

As the Revelation opens, the awesome Lord God, the Alpha and Omega
speaks. He is dressed as the Great High Priest, now in the true Holy of Holies.

Read the seven letters, noting each church's sins, along with the Lord's warnings, encouragements, and promises. Here we will especially focus on the last two letters, in the event that they represent the composite Church conditions nearest to His coming. The 7th, to the Laodicean church, seems to evoke vomiting!

> What promises does the Davidic Messianic King give Philadelphian church's overcomers?
> Revelation 3:10-13

> What are the "blind" Laodiceans' sins, and what counsel is given?
> Revelation 3:14-18

> To an individual who "hears and opens" his/her heart, what promises are given—one for while on earth, one in Heaven?
> Revelation 3:19-22

Scripture often reminds us: "Therefore, dear friends, since we already know this...." Remembering the "FFF" (three men on the wall) analogy, in light of the facts we put our faith in, how do we feel about "the last days"? That is, in light of what we trust to be true (because we trust the One who revealed these things) how should we incorporate what we *know* into our *doing*—our personal application?

> II Corinthians 3:18 to 5:10 wonderfully holds up reasons for not losing heart, and applies one "therefore" after another. Which most moves you?

<u>How might the dynamics in II Corinthians 3-5 be lived out at such a time as this?</u> First of all, our hearts must be right before God. Through trusting the person and saving work of the Lord Jesus for our redemption, believers each have peace with God, according to Romans 5:1. By living in union with Him, and being indwelt by the Spirit, we experience the peace of God, as Philippians 4:7 affirms. Once we get right with God, daily life then is lived in dependence upon Him. He will draw us into fellowship with believers, and plant in our hearts His deep concern for unbelievers. God's people also have a prophetic role to play in the wider world's "wheat and tares" societies.

<u>Prophetic foreshadowing</u>: God called Jeremiah to be a prophetic voice to the Old Covenant community when God was about to judge and discipline His unrepentant people through the Babylonian captivity. That judgment on Israel in microcosm warns us about God's approaching judgment in macrocosm on the whole world. For long centuries, our merciful Father has repeatedly drawn His wandering people to return into fellowship and then restored them. From the final judgment, however, there is no return or restoration. Jeremiah was hated in his generation. God's prophetic voices today are hated as well. *Yeshua* told his disciples, "All men will hate you because of me" (Matthew 10:21). Nevertheless, "overcoming" is His challenge to the seven churches. We must be clear that overcoming is not something we do; it is something we cooperate with the Holy Spirit's doing in and through us.

<u>The call to Messianic living</u>. We need the long view, remembering the scope and the end of the Messianic story. We know that *Yeshua* the Messiah has already won the victory over sin and death, and that we are sharing in

that victory. He promises to return in glory to bring in a new Heaven and new earth—a whole new creation minus sin and death and blessed with righteousness and renewed fellowship. Matthew 24:14 gives us a clue to the timing of His return, and identifies our primary task until He comes. Meanwhile, pressures on God's people, and on the world, are intensifying as the Day approaches.

Principles for this generation's calling: We've been given Biblical guidelines that the Spirit of God can actualize in each believer and in our corporate community. We are each called personally to live thankfully, prayerfully, faithfully, and expectantly. Considering the wider world, we are also called to live redemptively, compassionately, and prophetically. Let's think about how these life choices might look now, in days similar to Jeremiah's time.

We are to live THANKFULLY. How marvelous to have been redeemed, to be indwelt and gifted by the Spirit of God, and to look forward to a marvelous future!

Paul pours out praises for amazing blessings which are also for believers today. Notice the verbs in Ephesians 1:3-16.

We are to live PRAYERFULLY. How wonderful to be invited to "come boldly to the throne of grace to find help in time of need" (Hebrews 4:16 RSV). How amazing that the Spirit interprets our prayers to God (Romans 8:26, 27).

How important is prayer declared to be in the spiritual warfare surrounding us? Ephesians 6:18-19

We are to live FAITHFULLY. "Faith comes by hearing the message, and the message is heard through the word of Christ" (Romans 10:17). The world's voices are deafening. Our indispensable offensive weapon is the Word of God (Ephesians 6:17). Every believer deeply needs to take in the Word of God day by day, in order to fellowship with our Lord, to grow, and to overcome.

Overcoming requires fullness of faith in our Lord, trusting Him to do in us what we are unable to do.

How did *Yeshua* explain this necessity in John 15:1-8?

We are to live EXPECTANTLY. In spite of world chaos and the strong delusion which is blanketing our own country, our focus is to be on God's final victory, in which the faithful will share. Things seem to be falling apart, but knowing what the Bible predicts, they also seem to be falling into place. Pieces of the prophetic puzzle are fitting together. Although suffering and widespread martyrdom are on our horizon, our role is to stand firm and keep looking up. The King is coming!

What expectations and encouragements do we find in II Thessalonians 2:9-17, and I Thessalonians 4:13-18?

We are to live REDEMPTIVELY. God's plan for man's redemption is at the heart of the Bible's whole story. What did the Savior come to do? God's goal is to redeem humanity and restore fellowship. Therefore God's people's primary task is to present the Gospel of Jesus the Christ to the whole world. That goal requires God's people to get the message of salvation to every tribe, people, and nation.

What was the risen Messiah's final command?
Matthew 28:18-20

Therefore what are those "in Christ" to do?
II Corinthians 5:14-21

What clue to completion did our Lord give?
Matthew 24:14

We are to live COMPASSIONATELY. People wedded to God's heart feel for those around them, and even those far away who are hurting. Therefore the Body of Christ is motivated to let God work through us to help heal the world's hurts—physical, emotional, and most important into eternity, spiritual. In difficult times, needs will be intensifying. Those of us who are reading the signs of the times need to be prepared to offer people comfort, help, prayer, Biblical counsel, and physical assistance. We'd be wise to think ahead about what might be needed in an emergency. Although we have a firm confidence that keeps us from crippling concern, people around us in chaotic times may be overcome with fear, confusion, and the lack of physical necessities. It seems prudent to have a few provisions on hand to keep strong and be able to help others in times of catastrophe. Imagine a situation when your home and your neighbors' have lost all electricity, light, heat, telephone and computer connections; and services are all closed, such as grocery stores, gas stations, and banks. What might you wish you had on hand, at least for a few hours or days? What spiritual resources would you need to store up within yourself to call upon, and what spiritual resources would you want to be able to share?

Your ideas?

We are to live PROPHETICALLY. Far from being wild-eyed fanatics, sober Biblical Christians have the natural obligation to warn unsuspecting people to get their spiritual households in order in times like these. We don't make new pronouncements; we simply inform them from the Scriptures. We are not vindictive as we warn about judgment; we are heartbroken that people we love, and people we don't even know, are oblivious to their danger. Many church goers even seem to either be asleep or else they disregard *Yeshua*'s repeated admonitions: "Watch!"

> How seriously do you think He meant His "watch" commands?
> Matthew 24:42-44, Mark 13:32-37, and Luke 12:35-40

> What does our "longing for His appearing" seem to mean to Him?
> II Timothy 4:8

Three serious pitfalls obscure our understanding of God's prophetic message. Our lack of vision hinders prophetic living. Deep problems in Christendom cripple people's understanding of salvation history. How so? First, many believers have a weak background in the Old Testament. Secondly, few grasp the unity and continuity of the Old and New Testament. Furthermore, many Christians have inherited unbiblical attitudes toward God's chosen people. Let's look at the three more carefully.

First, the Old Testament's historical sections provide insight into God's dealings with humanity, and His prophetic messages express His heart. The Law, Tabernacle and Feasts of the Hebrew *Torah* provide a foundation for understanding God's way of living, way of worship, and way of timing (His calendar). These foundations are invaluable for understanding the whole story of redemption.

❖ ACTION: Old Testament studies are valuable, such as G. Campbell Morgan's *The Unfolding Message of the Bible*, and C.H. Mackintosh's *Genesis to Deuteronomy*. Appendix B and C provide thumbnail sketches of the Tabernacle and the Feasts, taken from the author's short Old Testament-based study, *All*, and the more extensive study, **The Messiah Mystery**.

Second, seeing the indivisible connection between the two covenants (recorded in the Old and New Testaments) is fundamental for understanding God's historical progression toward the goal of history. If all that we teach to children and even to adults are only colorful stories from the Old Testament, "sound bites," and not the whole counsel of God, we leave people ill prepared to grasp or cooperate with God's plan for redeeming mankind.

❖ ACTION: For instance, try summarizing the message of God to man (the Bible) as you understand it in one page or less. Thinking panoramically about the Bible helps us to be a better witness and a more effective Bible teacher of any age group. This would require careful thinking, some study, and a time investment. Add your personal testimony to its reality. Pray about sharing a short form of this with someone the Spirit would lead you to, and for the courage to do so.

Third, as early as the 2nd Century, Church fathers began developing unbiblical attitudes toward Jewishness. The trajectory led to a Gentilized theology, seeing the Church as replacing Israel—i.e. "superseding" God's chosen people. The Biblical injunction that "the branch should not boast above the root" (Romans 11:17, 18) was forgotten. Gratitude waned for the spiritual treasure house we received from our Jewish patriarchs, prophets, and apostles. Having dismissed Israel as "finished," anti-Semitism developed and often surfaced. Evil as horrendous as the Holocaust grew out of Christendom's misguided stance toward Judaism. Study 7 examined this tragic triumph of Satan's hatred. Significantly, today's budding Messianic Movement is causing the Church to re-evaluate its unbiblical position now that Jewish believers in *Yeshua* as Messiah are multiplying. World events are whirling around

Jerusalem as well. Israel has a future, according to the Prophets, as indicated in Romans 11:25-32, and as recorded in Revelation.

❖ ACTION: How can our congregations be helped to correct our tragic Jew/Gentile divisions? Awareness, repentance, and prayer are good beginnings. Israel in today's world is threatened with another Holocaust. Christians worldwide are beginning to face similar situations. In the Middle East, God's enemy is capitalizing on sins and jealousies that date back to Abraham's day, but are affecting the wider world. Awakening to these generationally-inherited realities is an urgent necessity today. *(Appendix F lists resources that inform and awaken us to this age-old rift in need of healing.)*

God's Kingdom will come! "In the meantime," many are suffering. Perpetrators of evil and hatred are exacting a high price from multitudes of our brothers and sisters all over the world today. Revelation 7 reveals martyrs from many tribes and nations who come out of the great tribulation (Revelation 7:9, 13-14).

Israel appears to be at the center of things in the last days. Notice that Revelation is full of Jewish/Gentile references. The "root" and "branches" appear—144,000 sealed Jewish people, and "every nation, tribe, people, and nation"—largely Gentiles. "Jerusalem" appears repeatedly, always at the center, whether in cataclysms, or final restoration.

What do we learn about these two communities from Romans 11:25-29?

Root and branches are "one new man" in *Yeshua* (Ephesians 2:11-22). Our Lord is fundamentally our mutual root. Furthermore even if there have been divisions throughout history, today's various enemies of the God of Abraham, Isaac, and Jacob class Israel and the Christian world together. Like it or not, the two covenant peoples are called to appreciate and support each another as the Day approaches.

In the meantime, we will be strengthened by keeping His eternal perspective as we live out our Lord's faithfulness until He comes.

♥ *And me?*

What practical steps am I convicted to take as I try to be ready like a "wise virgin" (Matthew 25:1-13) during our long wait for the Bridegroom? Where do I intend to get sufficient oil?

Prayer:

We look with Jude 24, 25 in worship to God: "To him who is able to keep you from falling and to present you before his glorious presence without fault and with great joy—to the only God our Savior be glory, majesty, power and authority, through Jesus Christ our Lord, before all ages, now and forevermore. Amen."

Ω

THEREFORE FIX YOUR EYES ON JESUS

Therefore, since we are surrounded by such a great cloud of witnesses, let us throw off everything that hinders and the sin that so easily entangles, and let us run with perseverance the race marked out for us. Let us fix our eyes on Jesus, the author and perfecter of our faith, who for the joy set before him endured the cross, scorning its shame, and sat down at the right hand of the throne of God. Consider him who endured such opposition from sinful men, so that you will not grow weary and lose heart.

Hebrews 12:1-3

Appendix A
Foreshadowing in the Word

Exodus, Leviticus, Numbers, Deuteronomy
Luke 24:25-27

Messiah's fulfillment of the Tabernacle
Messiah's fulfillment of the Feasts

Foundational to a full understanding of God's message and ways, are the patterns He carefully laid out at Mt. Sinai at the initiation of His Covenant with the people He had chosen to work through. The Tabernacle is a foreshadowing in space, and the Feasts are a foreshadowing in time, of His panoramic plan to save the world through the Messiah.

Yeshua the Messiah came to dwell ("tabernacle") among us (John 1:14). Every aspect of the Tabernacle had pointed to Him. Now Jesus is our living Tabernacle. The Holy Spirit indwells His people, who are now "tabernacles" for His dwelling on earth. Understanding and appreciating the Tabernacle in the Old Testament is vital for grasping the depths of meaning related to fulfillments of our Lord. *(See Appendix C for more about this.)*

Furthermore, God's whole plan for Time laid out in His Feast pattern in the *Torah*, gives us priceless keys for understanding Yeshua's teaching, ministry, interactions, and fulfillments. The Feasts are also eschatological, helping us understand the progression of history. Many wonderful resources for studying the Tabernacle and Feasts are available. *(See Appendix B and C.)*

The next few pages taken from the author's previously published study, "*All*," provide small glimpses into the riches of these things. "*All*" is the summary word referring to Yeshua's revelation to the two who met Him the evening of the Resurrection on the road to Emmaus, to whom He said:

> "How foolish you are and how slow of heart to believe all that the prophets have spoken. Did not the Christ have to suffer these things and then enter his glory?" And beginning with Moses and all the Prophets, he explained to them what was said in all the Scriptures concerning himself (Luke 24:25-27).

Appendix B

The Feasts

Why Study the Feasts?

For all believers in *Yeshua*, the Feasts are so built into Jesus' engagement with His culture and His fulfillments in the New Testament that we cannot understand the whole counsel of God without understanding the Feasts. Furthermore, the Feasts provide for the Church one of God's primary teaching tools that inform us about His plan for history, whether looking back at His prefiguring or forward to His predicting. The Feasts provide clues to understanding the progression of His eschatological purposes across the ages.

For Messianic Jews, the Feasts were part of their original Covenant with God, and comprise great swaths of their history. Their wider community is still celebrating the Feasts in their homes and synagogues, so these are times of fellowship and possible witness.

For Gentile Christians, the question arises, " Why would Israel's Feasts unto the Lord be of importance to Gentile Christians in the Church, since the Feasts are Jewish, are in the past, and seemingly not part of the New Covenant?" Below are some reasons.

1. Every Christian needs to understand the Jewish culture, Whatever their nationality, Gentiles need to be bi-cultural to understand the Scriptures, our Jewish roots, and our Jewish Messiah. God chose to reveal His plan for the world through a particular people, so that the rest of us might have a real-life account of His interactions with His "seed" community—the Old Covenant community.

2. The Feasts are an all-pervading part of God's people's whole societal structure. At Mt. Sinai, God moved His people from slavery to nationhood. He gave Israel her history, deliverer, laws, ordinances, worship, priesthood, geography, agricultural rhythms, calendar, ceremonies, attitudes, and identity. Understanding the seasons of God's year brings remarkable clarity to the study of Scripture.

3. The New Testament bases spiritual truth upon the Old Testament, continually appealing to it, in hundreds of passages. All of Scripture was written for our instruction (II Tim. 3:16). The larger portion is the Old Testament—the Scripture Jesus and the Disciples used. If we miss the foundation of those meanings, we are kept from deeply appreciating their outworking and fulfillment. Grasping these connections builds faith in the God who so intricately devised and timed the plan that He has been working out.

4. The Messiah's life happenings were perfectly timed in conjunction with the celebration of the Feasts. Our Jewish Messiah repeatedly framed His teachings in the language of the Feasts. The Tabernacle and celebration of the Feasts provided a platform, an audience, and timing that foreshadowed and heightened the meaning of the Messiah's birth, life, death, and resurrection.

5. It is natural for the waiting Bride to look for the Bridegroom's promised return in relation to the Feasts. The Scriptures end with the Spirit and the Bride's cry, "Come Lord Jesus!" The major events of the Messiah's life took place in exact relation to the first four. (Sacrifice at Passover and Unleavened Bread, Resurrection on First Fruits, the Gift of the Holy Spirit given on Pentecost.) It is reasonable for expectant believers to wait with faith, examining the meaning and promise of the Fall Feasts (Trumpets, Atonement, and Tabernacles).

6. Today's world events spin around Israel, the clock and geo-center of history. God's Word promises a future, still, for Israel. Jewish and Christian believers in the Messiah, whether in Israel or abroad, are being drawn into the situation. Brothers and sisters are concerned about all of God's beloved world: the Messianic remnant, His still unbelieving Chosen People, and the Gentile ethnic groups yet to be reached. The Messiah's community is called to be alert in "such a time as this."

Q. HOW SHALL WE LEARN ABOUT THE FEASTS? Some ways:

➤ By studying them throughout the Bible—from their institution in Exodus, to Revelation. C.H. Mackintosh's *Genesis through*

Deuteronomy is one valuable resource. *The Messiah Mystery* has two chapters on "The Messiah and the Feasts." Many books on the Feasts are available.

➢ By getting a clear grasp of the relationship between the Old Testament Passover Feast and the New Testament Lord's Supper observance. The Rosens' *Christ in the Passover* is one classic resource.

➢ By joining Jewish friends in their Passover Seder celebrations, their Sabbath evening, and other Feasts.

➢ By praying for the unbelieving Jewish community, especially on Yom Kippur, as we await their eventual awakening.

➢ By experimenting with the Feasts by seeing them celebrated (a Jewish-led Seder, for instance) or by celebrating them as Gentiles, using guides available, such as Seder booklets (*Haggadahs*), or helps like Martha Zimmerman's *Celebrating Biblical Feasts.*

CAUTIONS!

Not to become "Judaized," humanly preferring OT Torah laws to faith.
Not to become "puffed up," thinking one knows more than others.
Not to become obsessed with the attractiveness and fascination of Jewish culture.
Not to be blinded by God's Enemy's use of the persecutions of history, to destroy.
Not to break fellowship with the yet unperfected blood-bought Bride.
Not to be detoured from our major assignment "until the end shall come."

The Feasts on the Biblical Calendar

Where are God's "Feasts unto the Lord" commanded? The Feasts are the subject of Exodus 12 (Passover's basic text), Exodus 23:14-17; Leviticus 16, 23, 25; Numbers 28, 29, Deuteronomy 16, and more.

When were they celebrated? The seven feasts were celebrated within the three seasons specified in Exodus 23:14. (Seven seems to be God's clue word for "complete.") In contrast to the solar calendar, God's calendar is lunar (timed with the moon – festivals usually at full moon – helpful with no electricity!).

WEEKLY FEAST: the Sabbath.
ANNUAL FEASTS circle the seasons by the agricultural rhythms.
Spring Feasts:
1. *Pesach* – Passover – 14th day of lst month
2. Unleavened Bread – I week concurrent with Passover
3. First Fruits – the first Sunday after Passover
Summer begins: Feast 50 days after First Fruits:
4. *Shavuot* - Feast of Weeks (7 x 7 + 1= 50), or Pentecost
Fall Feasts:
5. *Rosh Hashanah* – Trumpets – lst day of 7th month
6. *Yom Kippur* – Day of Atonement – 10th day of 7th month (a fast)
7. *Sukkot* – Ingathering, or Tabernacles, or Booths – 15th day of 7th month for a week, followed by an "8th day" (new beginning) feast

WHOLE YEAR FEASTS:
1. The *Shmitah* – the Sabbatical year – every 7th year – the land is to rest and all consumer debts are to be canceled.

2. The *Yovel* – the JUBILEE year – every 50th year – the land is to rest, all land is to be returned to the original owners, and the mortgages are canceled.

7TH year LAND REST, and 7 x 7 + 1= 50 JUBILEE YEAR: Leviticus 25

Visualizing the Feasts According to the Agricultural Cycle

(Exodus.23:14-17; Leviticus 23:5, 15-16, 33)

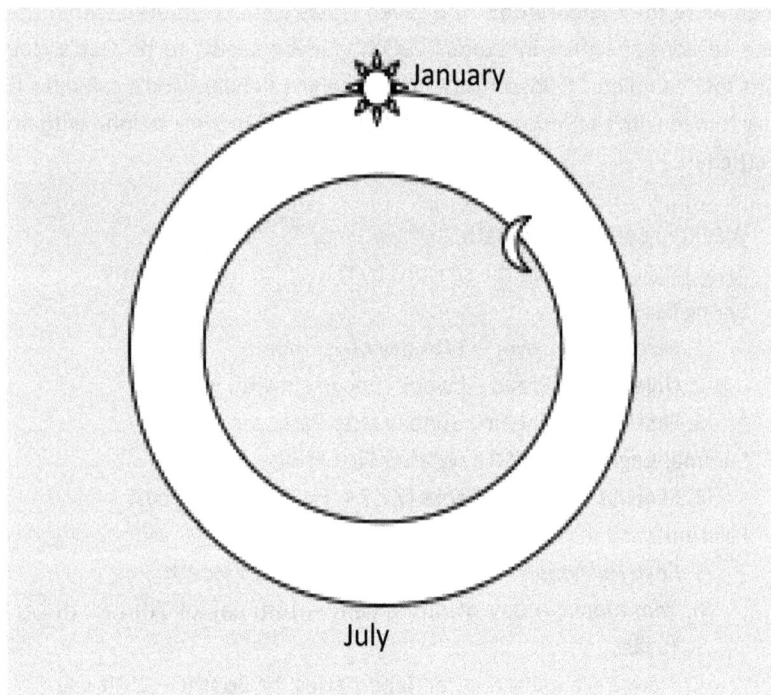

Write it in: On the outer circle above, mark "Jan., Feb.," etc. for the solar month, clockwise. On the inner circle, place a symbol for each annual feast on its approximate Hebrew lunar month. Passover starts on the 14th of the Hebrew lunar first month (solar March/April), Tabernacles on the 15th of the seventh month (solar Sept. /Oct.).

Visualizing the Feasts by the Yearly "Remembering"

1.Passover – saved from death, delivered, freed from bondage

2.Unleavened Bread – hurried to escape and cross sea miraculously

3.First Fruits – arose out of Red Sea, delivered alive

4.Feast of Weeks – given the Law at Mt. Sinai

5.Trumpets – warning of judgment

6. Day of Atonement – blood taken into Tabernacle's Holy of Holies yearly

7. Tabernacles – remembered dwellings in the wilderness, harvests in the Land

Feasts were "teaching platforms." (See Exodus 23:15.) Understanding these dates and happenings at deeply cultural occasions can help open the Scriptures. Related to which Feast did each of these events occur?

_____ Crossing the Jordan, memory stones, and circumcision:
          Joshua 4:19-5:10

_____ King Solomon's celebration at the First Temple's dedication:
          I Kings 8

_____ Ezra reads the Law to the Israelites after the captivity:
          Nehemiah 8:1-12

Visualizing the Feasts Historically (an Eschatological View)

✝

ETERNITY (former days) 1 2 3 ❙ 4 (latter days) 5 6 7 ETERNITY

TIME

———————————————————————————➤

<u>Spring Feasts: completed during Incarnation and 50 days later:</u>

1 Passover: Jesus' sacrificial death

2. Unleavened Bread: His burial

3. First Fruits: His resurrection

4. Pentecost: Holy Spirit poured out on believers

(Summer: sowing & reaping – "the Times of the Gentiles")

<u>Fall Feasts: uncompleted, promised, and expected:</u>

5. Trumpets: Jesus' promised return

6. Day of Atonement: Israel sees "whom they have pierced"

7. Tabernacles: the final Ingathering of all believers

Cross lines on this chart, matching summer & each unfinished feast on the left with Scriptures on the right:

(Summer)	Zechariah 12:10, Revelation 1:7
5. Trumpets	I Thess. 4:16-17, I Cor. 15:51-52
6. Day of Atonement	Romans 11:25, Matthew. 24:14
7. Tabernacles	Zechariah 14:16-17, Rev. 21:3

See if you can list the Feasts in order and tell what time of year they occur and their significance.

Appendix C

The Tabernacle

The Tabernacle and Temple's Intricate Foreshadowing of Messiah Yeshua's Indentity, Work, and Significance

The Bible gives us a rich vein of prophetic foreshadowing through God's careful directions for creating His people's single place of worship—the Tabernacle (when they were traveling), and the Temple (when they were settled in the Land).

God's specific directions to build the Tabernacle "exactly like the pattern I will show you" (Exodus 25:9) were eventually revealed to find their prophetic fulfillment in exact matchings of God's pattern to the Person and work of Messiah *Yeshua* when He arrived.

In the New Testament, the book of Hebrews explains that these patterns were shadows of realities in Heaven (Hebrews 10:1). The Tabernacle was an earthly copy of a Heavenly reality (Hebrew 8:5).

A thumbnail sketch and visual of the Tabernacle's elements follow. Its dimensions, placements, and seven articles are pictured in this Appendix C and can be exactly matched with our Lord's fulfillments. These clear convergences provide deep study material. Volumes have been written about the spiritual treasures deposited in the Tabernacle. (Among others, valuable written and pictorial resources available are Henry William Solteau's *The Tabernacle and The Holy Vessels* and *Furniture of the Tabernacle*, Kregel Publications. Two chapters of the Bascoms' *The Messiah Mystery* are on the Messiah and the Tabernacle.)

For our purposes, this storehouse of revelation (of Yeshua's identity and our relationship with Him) can be viewed from a number of viewpoints. Here are three:

➢ Uncovering its elements in relationship to the Messiah's identity.
➢ Employing its elements as a pattern for entering into His salvation.
➢ Enjoying its elements as a pattern for worshipping Him.

The following outlines look like insignificant listings on paper. Yet if earnestly pursued and received from the Spirit, our greater appreciation for our Lord and our appropriation of His truths can leap light years ahead. *(The next two pages include visuals that will be helpful.)*

Visualizing Tabernacle elements related to the Messiah's identity:

The pure white curtain around the outside of the Tabernacle separating those inside from the world reminds us that we are called to be "in the world but not of it."

The Tabernacle has only one entrance which reminds us that Yeshua said He is the door (John 10:9) and that "no one comes to the Father except through Me" (John 14:6).

The Tabernacle's four coverings are non-descript on top, but most beautiful within. This brings to mind Isaiah 53:2b "He had no beauty or majesty to attract us to him, nothing in his appearance that we should desire him." Yet to know Him is the most beautiful experience ever.

The Shekinah glory cloud of God's Presence rising above the Holy of Holies foreshadows God's presence dwelling within us through the Holy Spirit.

People come into the outer court; only priests enter inside where curtains veil the Holy Place, and the Most Holy Place, which shows that the Father wants intimacy with us each individually alone—those whom He has made to be the priesthood of believers (I Peter 2:9).

The Tabernacle Details

Then have them make a sanctuary for me, and I will dwell among them. Make this tabernacle and all its furnishings exactly like the pattern I will show you. – Exodus 25:8-9

Tabernacle "pattern "– seven articles, dimensions, construction, materials: Exodus 25-27 and 35-38.

THE TABERNACLE VIEWED FROM THE OUTSIDE:
A. Linen fence around the courtyard – (100x50 cubits): Exodus 27:9-19
B. Curtained entrances to the courtyard and the Holy Place
C. Priests, Levites, animals, and people participating in sacrifices
D. Tabernacle (15x45 feet or 10x30 cubits) with four layers of coverings
E. The *Shekinah* glory cloud rising from above the Mercy Seat (not in graphic)
Two articles visible in the courtyard outside: Exodus 27:9-19
  1. The Brazen Altar for *burnt sacrifices*: Exodus 27:1-8*
  2. The Laver for *washing*: Exodus 38:8
* Offerings were to be made at only one place: Deuteronomy 12:1-14.

INSIDE THE TABERNACLE:
(Structure made of acacia wood planks covered with gold, held up with rings and bars; curtains in front of the Holy Place and Most Holy Place.)

The Holy Place – seen only by priests and Levites, daily
  3. The Golden seven-flame Lampstand, for light: Ex. 25:31-40
  4. The Bread of the Presence, for representation: Ex. 25:23-30
  5. The Golden Incense Altar, for intercession: Ex. 37:25-29
The Most Holy Place – seen only by the High Priest, yearly
  6. The Ark of the Covenant, holding the Law: Ex.25:10-16
  7. The Mercy Seat, the throne of grace: Ex. 25:17-22

On the accompanying drawing, pencil in letters and numbers at their specified locations for these aspects:

 A-E: the visible aspects from outside (listed above)

 1-7: the articles (listed above) used in Tabernacle worship

What happened at the first erection of the Tabernacle at Mt. Sinai? (Exodus 40:34-35)

TABERNACLE (without its four coverings)

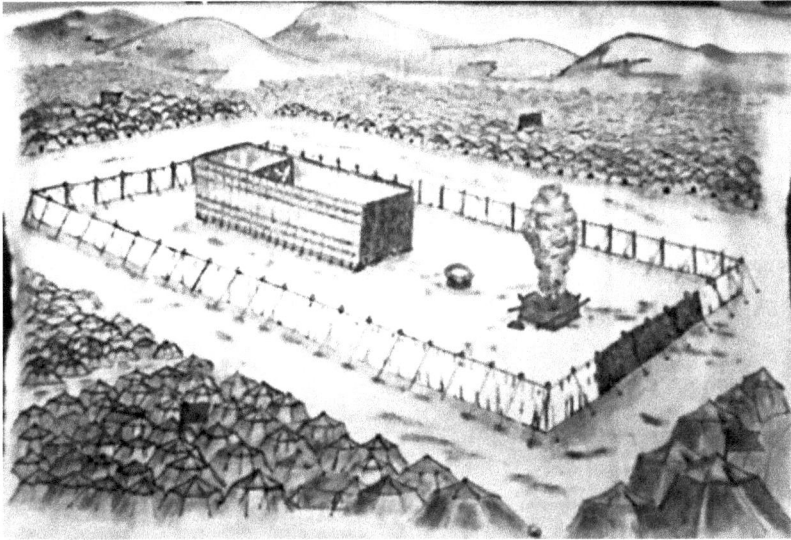

TRIBAL CAMPS: EAST: Moses, Aaron, and Levites, plus Zebulun, Judah, Issachar. SOUTH: Simeon, Reuben, Gad. WEST: Benjamin, Ephraim, Manasseh. NORTH: Asher, Dan, Naphtali.

(The *Shekinah* glory cloud is not shown in this graphic.)

TABERNACLE DRAWING: (top is north)

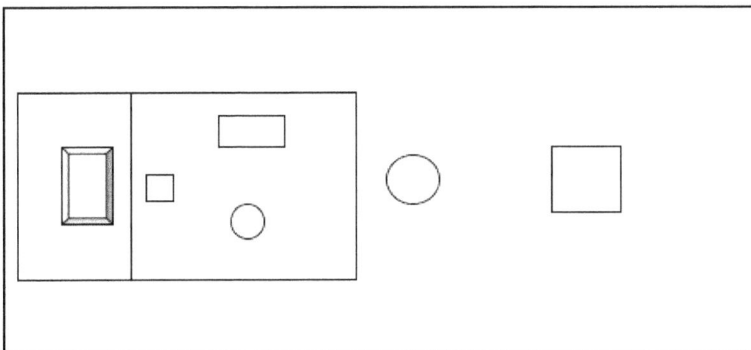

ALL SACRIFICES, AND ISRAEL'S FEASTS UNTO THE LORD were to be celebrated at the Tabernacle, and later at the Temple, in Jerusalem.

Exodus records the Law and reveals God's Tabernacle pattern (25-40).

Leviticus describes the priesthood, sacrifices, and Feasts (23-25).

Numbers records Tabernacle's movements, and Feast teachings (9, 28, 29).

Deuteronomy recounts the Law and lists the Feasts (16).

Tracing Tabernacle Meanings Throughout the New Testament:

The True Tabernacle

Its location:
Hebrews 8:1-2
Hebrews 8:5
Hebrews 9:22-24
Revelation 11:19

The Seven Articles of the Tabernacle

Courtyard with only one entrance: John 14:6
Shekina Glory Cloud: Visible sign of the Divine Presence:
Exodus 40:34-38

1st Article: Altar of Sacrifice:
Romans 4:25
Hebrews 9:26-27
Hebrews 10: 4, 12
I John 2: 2

2nd Article: Laver of Cleansing:
I Corinthians 1:30 RSV
II Thessalonians 2:13
I Peter 1:2

Hebrews 9:14

I John 1:9

Holy Place: Opened to the Priesthood of believers:

I Peter 2:5

Revelation 5:10

3rd Article: Seven-flame Menorah Light

John 1:4, 9

John 8:12, 9:5

Revelation 21:23

4th Article: Bread of the Presence

John 6:35

John 6:48-51

Matthew 14:18-21

Luke 22:19

I Corinthians 11:23-24

5th Article: Incense Altar

Luke 6:12

John 17:1-26

Hebrews 5:7

Hebrews 13:15

Most Holy Place (Holy of Holies):

Great High Priest's yearly entering the Holy of Holies:

Hebrews 4:14-15

Hebrews 7:25

Hebrews 9: 11, 12

Dividing curtain rent when Messiah died:

Matthew 27:51

Hebrews 10:19

6th Article: Ark of the Covenant

Romans 3:20,

Romans 5:20-21

7th Article: Mercy Seat (Exodus 25:22)

Hebrews 4:16

Hebrews 6:19

God has emphasized the Tabernacle for His own purposes!

The foundations in Exodus, Leviticus, Numbers, and Deuteronomy amplify various aspects of the Tabernacle with teachings about the priesthood, sacrifices, feasts, and reiterations. The New Testament reveals *Yeshua's* fulfilling of it all. It has been estimated that Tabernacle teachings are found in over fifty chapters of the Bible.

Assimilation for the seriously searching disciple:

These Tabernacle-related Scriptures are vital to write down, realize, apply, and keep in memory. Tabernacle facts are like a many-faceted gem displaying the glory of God in the face of Jesus Christ (II Corinthians 4:6). As you look up Tabernacle-related Scriptures, imagine discovering them as if you were coming to them from various viewpoints:

- ✓ As a Messianic believer in 100 AD, with the Temple gone.
- ✓ As an untaught pagan convert to Christos in Asia Minor.
- ✓ As a searching American agnostic today.
- ✓ As yourself.

Appendix D

Visualizing the Word

Luke 24:25-27, John 17:20-26, Ephesians 1:3-14

All: Messiah's Old Covenant roles illustration

In: Faceted gem of "inness" illustration

A picture can communicate an idea in a way that is simple to understand. Illustrations that follow can be aids in connecting spiritual concepts with visual images. The two "gems" summarize *All* and *In*.

(The following illustrations and verse collections originated in former studies by the author, called All and In. The Therefore studies refer to these teachings and concepts as well, in a more abbreviated form.)

All: Luke 24:25-27

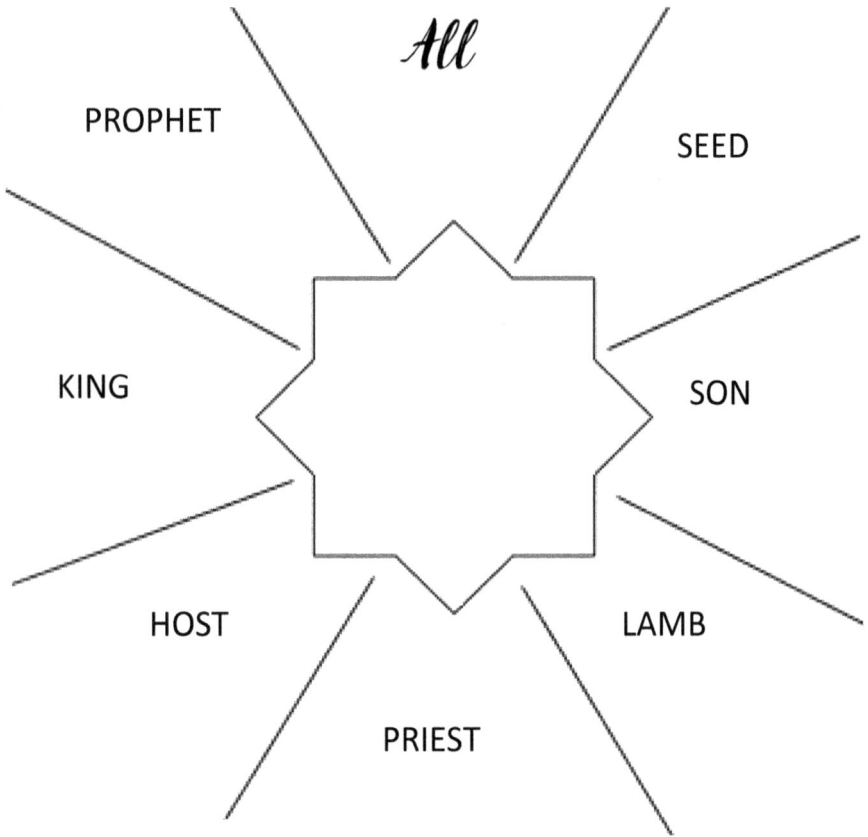

All

PROPHET

SEED

KING

SON

HOST

LAMB

PRIEST

*THE MESSIAH'S
OLD COVENANT ROLES
PICTURED AS
FACETS OF THE MESSIANIC GEM*

Read from 1:00 clockwise, moving through "Moses and the prophets" – the Old Testament – from Genesis to Malachi. Correlate the Gem Illustration above with Appendix E Key Verses. Together they demonstrate the Old and New Testaments' inseparable disclosure.

In: John 17:20-26, Ephesians 1:3-14

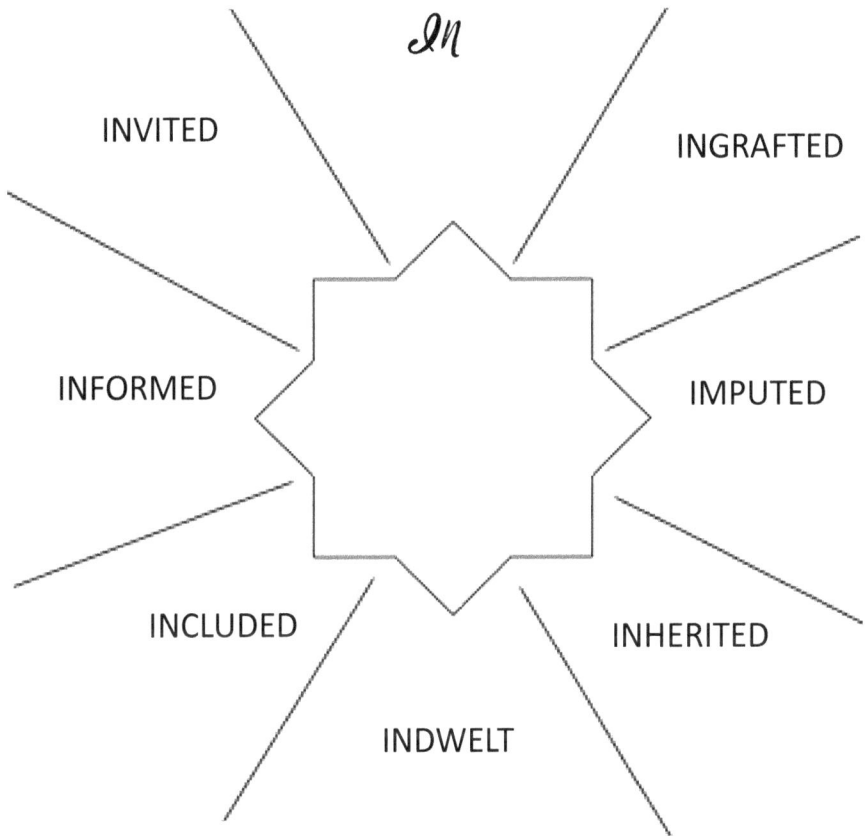

In

INVITED

INGRAFTED

INFORMED

IMPUTED

INCLUDED

INHERITED

INDWELT

*ASPECTS OF THE MESSIAH'S
NEW COVENANT
INCARNATION IN HIS PEOPLE
THROUGH THE OUTPOURED SPIRIT*

Read the above illustration from 1:00 clockwise. (After the Incarnation and Inauguration in the Gospels and Acts, "in's" can be gleaned throughout the Letters and Revelation.) Compare this illustration with the accompanying Key Verses in Appendix E.

Appendix E
Conserving the Word

II Timothy 3:16-17, II Peter 1:20-21

All Key Verses
IN Key Verses
Therefore Key Verses

Memorizing God's Word is a vital aid to the believer's spiritual life!

➢ It yields an exact and deepened grasp of Scripture's meaning.
➢ It imbeds it in our hearts, to be called up when especially needed.
➢ It helps us share God's Word specifically with others, helping them go to the Biblical source.
➢ Scripture hidden in the heart is a blessed presence when our Bible is not at hand, or may have been taken away from us.

KEYS TO All THE MESSIAH IS

SEED

For since death came through a man, the resurrection from the dead comes also through a man. For as in Adam all die, so in Christ all will be made alive.

I Corinthians 15:21-22

SON

By faith Abraham, when God tested him, offered Isaac as a sacrifice. He who had received the promises was about to sacrifice his one and only son, even though God had said to him, "It is through Isaac that your offspring will be reckoned." Abraham reasoned that God could raise the dead, and figuratively speaking, he did receive Isaac back from death.

Hebrews 11:17-19

LAMB

The next day John saw Jesus coming toward him and said, "Look, the Lamb of God, who takes away the sin of the world!"

John 1:29

PRIEST

When Christ came as high priest of the good things that are already here, he went through the greater and more perfect tabernacle that is not man-made, that is to say, not a part of this creation. He did not enter by means of the blood of goats and calves; but he entered the Most Holy Place once for all by his own blood, having obtained eternal redemption.

Hebrews 9:11-12

HOST

For Christ our Passover lamb has been sacrificed. Therefore let us keep the Festival, not with the old yeast, the yeast of malice and wickedness, but with bread without yeast, the bread of sincerity and truth.

I Corinthians 5:7b-8

KING

"I, Jesus, have sent my angel to give you this testimony for the churches. I am the Root and the Offspring of David, and the bright Morning Star."

Revelation 22:16

PROPHET

In the past God spoke to our forefathers through the prophets at many times and in various ways, but in these last days he has spoken to us by his son, through whom he made the universe.

Hebrews 1:1-2

ALL

He said to them, "how foolish you are, and how slow [of heart] to believe all that the prophets have spoken! Did not the Messiah have to suffer these things and then enter his glory?" And beginning with Moses and all the Prophets, he explained to them what was said in all the Scriptures concerning himself.

Luke 24:25-27 (NIV 2011)

KEYS TO BEING *IN* CHRIST

INTEGRATION

In the past God spoke to our forefathers through the prophets at many times and in various ways, but in these last days he has spoken to us by his Son, whom he appointed heir of all things, and through whom he made the universe.

Hebrews 1:1-2

INCLUDED

And you also were included in Christ when you heard the word of truth, the gospel of your salvation. Having believed, you were marked in him with a seal, the promised Holy Spirit, who is a deposit guaranteeing our inheritance until the redemption of those who are God's possession - to the praise of his glory. **Ephesians 1:13-14**

INCARNATION

In the beginning was the Word, and the Word was with God, and the Word was God. He was with God in the beginning. ...The Word became flesh, and made his dwelling among us. We have seen his glory, the glory of the One and Only, who came from the Father, full of grace and truth.

John 1:1, 2, 14

INDWELT

To them God has chosen to make known among the Gentiles the glorious riches of this mystery, which is Christ in you, the hope of glory.

Colossians 1:27

INAUGURATION

Exalted to the right hand of God, He has received from the Father the promised Holy Spirit and has poured out what you now see and hear.

Acts 2:33

INHERITED

For this reason Christ is the mediator of a new covenant, that those who are called may receive the promised eternal inheritance - now that he has died as a ransom to set them free from the sins committed under the first covenant. **Hebrews 9:15**

INGRAFTED

If some of the branches have been broken off, and you, though a wild olive shoot, have been grafted in among the others and now share in the nourishing sap from the olive root, do not boast over those branches. If you do, consider this: You do not support the root, but the root supports you.

Romans 11:17-18

INFORMED

"Do not be afraid. I am the First and the Last. I am the Living One; I was dead, and behold I am alive for ever and ever. And I hold the keys of death and Hades. Write, therefore, what you have seen, what is now and what will take place later." **Revelation 1:17b-19**

IMPUTED

Consider Abraham: "He believed God, and it was credited to him as righteousness." Understand, then, that those who believe are children of Abraham. The Scripture foresaw that God would justify the Gentiles by faith, and announced the gospel in advance to Abraham. "All nations will be blessed through you." So those who have faith are blessed along with Abraham, the man of faith.

Galatians 3:6-9

INVITED

Then the angel said to me, "Write: blessed are those who are invited to the wedding supper of the Lamb!" And he added, "These are the true words of God."

Revelation 19:9

Therefore KEY VERSES

THEREFORE SPEAK

It is written, "I believe; therefore I have spoken." With that spirit of faith we also believe and therefore speak, because we know that the one who raised the Lord Jesus from the dead will also raise us with Jesus and present us with you in his presence. All this is for your benefit, so that the grace that is reaching more and more people may cause thanksgiving to overflow to the glory of God.

II Corinthians 4:13-15

THEREFORE GOD EXALTED

Therefore God exalted him to the highest place and gave him the name that is above every name, that at the name of Jesus every knee should bow, in heaven and on earth and under the earth, and every tongue confess that Jesus Christ is Lord, to the glory of God the Father.

Philippians 2:9-11

THEREFORE
THE PROMISE GUARANTEED

Therefore, the promise comes by faith, so that it may be by grace and may be guaranteed to all Abraham's offspring – not only to those who are of the law but also to those who are of the faith of Abraham. He is the father of us all.

Romans 4:16

THEREFORE REMEMBER FORMERLY

Therefore, remember that formerly you who were Gentiles by birth and called "uncircumcised" by those who call themselves "the circumcision" (that done in the body by the hands of men) – remember that at that time you were separate from Christ, excluded from citizenship in Israel, and foreigners to the covenants of the promise, without hope and without God in the world. But now in Christ Jesus you who once were far away have been brought near through the blood of Christ.

Ephesians 2:11-13

THEREFORE LET US DRAW NEAR

Therefore brothers, since we have confidence to enter the Most Holy Place by the blood of Jesus, by a new and living way opened for us through the curtain, that is, his body, and since we have a great priest over the house of God, let us draw near to God with a sincere heart in full assurance of faith.

Hebrews 10:19-22a

THEREFORE JUSTIFIED

Therefore, my brothers, I want you to know that through Jesus the forgiveness of sins is proclaimed to you. Through him everyone who believes is justified from everything you could not be justified from by the Law of Moses.

Acts 13:38-39

THEREFORE CONSIDER

Consider therefore the kindness and sternness of God: sternness to those who fell, but kindness to you, provided that you continue in his kindness. Otherwise, you also will be cut off. And if they do not persist in unbelief, they will be grafted in, for God is able to graft them in again.

Romans 11:22-23

THEREFORE IMPLORE

We are therefore Christ's ambassadors, as though God were making his appeal through us. We implore you on Christ's behalf: Be reconciled to God.

II Corinthians 5:20

THEREFORE HUMBLE YOURSELVES

Humble yourselves, therefore, under God's mighty hand, that he may lift you up in due time. Cast all your anxiety on him, because he cares for you. Be self-controlled and alert. Your enemy the devil prowls around like a roaring lion looking for someone to devour. Resist him, standing firm in the faith because you know that your brothers throughout the world are undergoing the same kind of sufferings.

I Peter 5:6-9

THEREFORE ENCOURAGE EACH OTHER

For the Lord himself will come down from heaven, with a loud command, and with the voice of the archangel and with the trumpet call of God, and the dead in Christ will rise first. After that, we who are still alive and are left will be caught up together with them in the clouds to meet the Lord in the air. And so we will be with the Lord forever. Therefore encourage each other with these words.

I Thessalonians 4:16-18

THEREFORE DO NOT LOSE HEART

Therefore we do not lose heart. Though outwardly we are wasting away, yet inwardly we are being renewed day by day. For our light and momentary troubles are achieving for us an eternal glory that far outweighs them all. So we fix our eyes not on what is seen, but what is unseen. For what is seen is temporal, but what is unseen is eternal.

II Corinthians 4:16-18

THEREFORE FIX OUR EYES ON JESUS

Therefore, since we are surrounded by such a great cloud of witnesses, let us throw off everything that hinders and the sin that so easily entangles, and let us run with perseverance the race marked out for us. Let us fix our eyes on Jesus, the author and perfecter of our faith, who for the joy set before him endured the cross, scorning its shame, and sat down at the right hand of the throne of God. Consider him who endured such opposition from sinful men, so that you will not grow weary and lose heart.

Hebrews 12:1-3

Appendix F

Suggested Reading/Bibliography

Genesis 12:2-3; 17:7; Exodus 19:4-6; Romans 9-11

Resources Related to the Messianic Movement and
Jewish/Church Relationships:

Brown, Michael L., *Our Hands are Stained with Blood*, Destiny Image Publishers, Shippensburg, PA, 1992.

Buksbazen, Lydia, *They Looked for a City,* Friends of Israel Gospel Ministry, 9th edition, Bellmawr, NJ, 1955.

Gundry, Stanley N., Series Editor, *How Jewish is Christianity?*, Zondervan, Grand Rapids, Michigan, 2003.

Horner, Barry E, *Future Israel*, B&H Publishing Group, Nashville, Tennessee, 2007.

Jocz, Jakob, *The Jewish People and Jesus Christ after Auschwitz*, Baker Book House, Grand Rapids, MI, 1981.

Kehilah News Israel, a Messianic Israeli online newspaper, www. kehilanews.com. Accessed Aug. 2016.

Liberman, Paul, and Wasson, Jack, *Don't Call Me Christian*, Tishbite Press, Arlington, Texas, 2015.

Maoz Israel Report, an online and print Israeli magazine, www. maozisrael.com. Accessed Aug. 2016, http://www.maozisrael.org/ site/PageServer?pagename=maoz_report

McQuaid, Elwood, *The Zion Connection*, Harvest House Publishers, Eugene, Oregon, 1996.

Stern, David H., *Messianic Jewish Manifesto*, Jewish New Testament Publications, Jerusalem, Israel, l988.

Stern, David H., *Restoring the Jewishness of the Gospel*, Jewish New Testament Publications, Jerusalem, Israel, 1988.

Stern, David H., *The Complete Jewish Bible*, Jewish New Testament Publications, Clarksville, Maryland, l998.

Telchin, Stan, *Betrayed*, Chosen Books, Ada, Michigan, 2007.

The Messianic Times, a print and online newspaper: www.messianic times.com. Accessed Aug. 2016.

Vlach, Michael J., *Has the Church Replaced Israel?,* B&H Publishing Group, Nashville, Tennessee, 2010.

Wilson, Marvin R., *Our Father Abraham*, Wm B. Eerdmans Publishing Company, Grand Rapids, MI, 1989.

Zimmerman, Martha, *Celebrating the Biblical Feasts*, Bethany House Publishers, Ada, Michigan, 2004.

Reviews

"*Therefore* challenges us as followers of the Messiah to live in accordance to what we proclaim and consider all the ramifications of the Gospel. Kay Bascom's heart is for her students to see the Scriptures, both Jewish and Christian Testaments, as one grand story. Her panoramic approach to the Bible informs us that truth and action are the cause and effect of faith. I love that she does not shy away from the reality of persecution and sets our eyes heaven ward to look for Messiah's return. In light of these realities she concludes with seven principles of how we should therefore live."

--Teri Gasser, pastor's wife, writer, and speaker

If you desire a deeper understanding of God's redemption plan, as well as the role you play in it, then you will benefit from this book. *Therefore*, is not only a word study, but it's also a reminder of what is required of believers in response to what has been done for them. Bascom asks readers "to commit to examining the facts, [to] engaging his/her faith, and [to] conforming his/her life experience in response."

-- E. M. Gregory

Kay Bascom's THEREFORE study is a must for all believers. This study challenged me to deepen my walk with the Lord and truly study what He has done and continues to do among the Jewish people. Much of her study I had never encountered before and I did not even realize my own cultural misconceptions that I had bought into it until I dived into this study. Kay challenges the reader to think deeply about God's Word and to renew your heart and mind in alignment with His Scripture. I am truly changed and walking closer with the Lord as a result of this study and I highly recommend it for anyone who wants to grow deeper in the Word.

- Ashley Poland, a young mother

Thank you for studying with this *Therefore* Bible study. If it blessed you in any way, we would appreciate your taking a moment to write a review on Amazon, as well as on other sites like Barnes and Noble, Christian Book, Olive Press Publisher, and on social media. If we get 50 reviews on Amazon, then Amazon will include *Therefore* in their promotions, such as, "Customers who bought this item also bought...."

Thank you for helping this book get the exposure it needs!

To contact the author:

charlesnkbascom@gmail.com

The author's website:

www.messiahmysteryresources.org

Therefore

is available at:

olivepresspublisher.com

amazon.com

barnesandnoble.com

christianbook.com

and other online stores

Store managers:

Order wholesale through:

Ingram Book Company or

Spring Arbor

or by emailing:

olivepressbooks@gmail.com

www.ingramcontent.com/pod-product-compliance
Lightning Source LLC
Chambersburg PA
CBHW050013100426
42739CB00011B/2630